# ~Love Is~

*Get rid of all bitterness, rage and anger, brawling and slander, along with every form of malice. Be kind and compassionate to one another, forgiving each other, just as in Christ God forgave you.*

Ephesians 4:31-32

Love Is
MOFMCopyright©2019

ISBN-9781799070184
*"Books In Print*

Messages of Faith Ministry
dba Chaplaincy Nevada
P.O. Box 60215
Las Vegas Nevada 89160-1215
chaplaincynevada.org
*Author©Copyright2019*

Scripture quotations referenced from the Holy Bible.
*Resources include:*
The Holy Bible, Old Testament, New Testament, Webster,
NLT, NIV, New King James, and other translations.

# Introduction

## Love Is ~Las Vegas

*"Love the Lord your God with all your heart and with all your soul and with all your mind and with all your strength. The second: Love your neighbor as yourself, There is no command greater than these." Mark 12:30-31 NIV*

Las Vegas loves its neighbor.

Love is everyone who came together after the 1 October 2017 Harvest Festival Tragedy to give blood, feed the first responders, support the hospital staff, assist the injured, rescue and transport many survivors, sit with and pray for the loved ones and survivors (and many still do). People from around the world were a part of that music festival and in the true spirit of Las Vegas hospitality we helped them all. #VegasStronger

Love is everybody coming together and facilitating, and looking out for missing and exploited children to save them from the clutches of the dangerous streets and Human Traffickers.

Love is churches rotating hosting locations and ministers coming together in unity to pray for the needs of our communities, city, and state on daily, weekly and monthly basis.

Love Is everyone (the police, judges, elected officials, chaplains, ministers and community leaders ) working together to help reintegrate former inmates, teaching the skills they need to be successful citizens in society and to stay focused on becoming whole while serving our community after being released.

Love is the coauthors of this book "Love Is Heartwarming Memoirs from Las Vegas Chaplains "coming together to share their stories in the Chaplaincy Nevada third book in our anthology series.

It was a pleasure to work with our authors as they prepared their stories for you.

Each chaplain's story is unique and they tell you what "Love Is" through their eyes. God's Love is distinct and specific to each one of us. I know you will be encouraged. Enjoy our compilation and Thank you for supporting our ministry.

Tamia Dow
Senior Chaplain & Compiler

# Love Is

## Foreword

Love Is, a combination of testimonial stories written and compiled by nineteen Chaplain Writers.

Their personal narratives bring forth compelling portrayals of, heartbreak, brokenness, despair and miraculous accounts for successfully overcoming the hardships they encountered in life which either brought them into the love of Christ, or reinforced their faith and love in Christ.

*"And I slowly began to drift away from myself. I could see myself laying there in that hospital room. I could see the doctors and nurses attending to me. And then suddenly I was no longer there."*

# Love Is

## † Table of Contents †

# Senior Chaplain Tamia Dow

Tamia is a beloved child of God, a woman of faith who serves God, her community and her fellow (hu)man in many ways. She's a graduate from the University of Nevada Las Vegas with a Bachelor's Degree in Criminal Justice, a veteran of the US Army, and a retired Las Vegas Metropolitan Police Department Detective (1989-2012) .

Tamia is an award-winning international best-selling author and an award-winning filmmaker who creates faith based movies sharing her police experiences dealing with current cultural issues affecting our community.

Tamia is the compiler and coauthor of the Chaplaincy Nevada's book series which include ; "Faith Is Inspiring Stories from Las Vegas Chaplains " and "Jesus Is Transforming Testimonies Of Las Vegas Chaplains ". Her passion is empowering and educating people to live a life free from oppression and to live their life to their fullest calling. She speaks and conduct trainings worldwide in the area of living a God planned life, Leadership, Domestic Violence and Human Trafficking Prevention and Awareness.

Tamia graduated from Kairos School of Ministry through the International Church of Las Vegas and does global police and community outreaches/ missions. She serves as a Senior Chaplain, an Academy specialty instructor and a member of the Chaplain's Advisory Board with the Messages of Faith Ministries Chaplaincy Nevada. She also serves as a Police Consultant on the Adopt A Cop Nevada Advisory Board. She can be reached on Facebook and Twitter @ChaplainDow and at www.tamiadow.com

†Chapter One

# Love Is God's Grace

*By SR Chaplain Tamia Dow*

*For by grace you have been saved through faith. And this is not your own doing; it is the gift of God, not a result of works, so that no one may boast. Ephesians 2:8-9 ESV*

It was a clear sunny day as I raced my cousin Anthony on our 10 speed bikes. I had borrowed my cousin's bike which was made for a boy, so I rode standing tall while avoiding the middle bar on the bike.

I was catching up to Anthony as we rounded the corner near the pharmacy at Jefferson Avenue and Ferry. We were both focused on our race, not the traffic.

I almost had him. I was so close when I heard the vehicle's loud horn and looked over to my left to see a delivery truck heading right for my bike as I was coming off the curb between cars on to East Ferry Street. I gasped.

As if the hand of God himself had reached out, thankfully I was miraculously pushed aside closer to the curb where there were no cars parked. I watched the truck go by avoiding a collision; which seemed impending once I heard the horn.

I stopped my bike in shock and looked across the street at my cousin who was so focused on his winning the race that he hadn't seen the close encounter I had just experienced. I knew that was the hand of God protecting me. At that moment I knew I had a call on my life. I knew I should have been a hood ornament for that truck, except that was not God's plan.

As a faithful Catholic girl I knew God had done a miracle. Decades later, I vividly remember the incident. I also know God's grace and protection is real. I know that God will not allow us to be taken from this world before we have fulfilled our assigned mission. Not until we have completed our God given assignment.

Fast forward years later and another vivid memory of God's hand comes to my mind. While working graveyard as a police officer I was the third officer to arrive on a loud noise complaint. When I arrived my partners had people sitting in the living room discussing the dispute they were having.

There were three different parties involved. One was sitting in a recliner with a long black duster coat, a black tee shirt and jeans. After talking to my partner, Craig (name changed) I asked him if that person needed to be interviewed. He said yes. I asked Craig, who was actually my senior officer, if the subject had been patted down. Craig told me "don't worry about it he's good."

I had him stand up and walk in front of me into the front yard of the house so that when I interviewed him the other parties could not hear my interview.

As we got into the front yard the hairs on the back of my neck began to stand up. I felt that there was something off with this character. I told him, "I want to talk to you and get your side of the story but I do need to pat you down for my personal safety to ensure that you don't have any weapons."

As I began the pat him down I asked, "you do not have any weapons do you?" He turned his head over his shoulder to speak to me as I stood behind him, and he said "yes ma'am, I have a loaded 38 in the small of my back."

I immediately handcuffed him because of the amount of clothing he had on. I wanted to ensure that I was able to safely remove the weapon and that he was not able to gain access to it. After doing that and securing the weapon, Craig who had told me the guy was OK, walked out and saw the extra weapon in my duty belt.

Craig was a senior officer, and a "trainer" for junior officers. His face was red and he became enraged. Craig walked up and got in the face of the man who I had taken the gun from and said "Dude I asked you if you had any weapons!"

Craig was heated. I know he was upset because he missed the threat and had told me I would be ok with the suspect. I thank God for the divine insight to double check for all of our safety.

This happened early in my career, and definitely shaped my officer safety. Every time I arrived on the scene I made sure that any suspect or citizen that warranted or could pose a safety threat to the officers on scene was patted down before interviews and information were gathered.

I do know that was also God's hand protecting me.
 God's grace and favor.

We used to have a saying "God looks out for Fools and Cops". I know most first responders have an "oh crap" testimony they can share about when they could have been killed or injured if God had not protected them and their partners.

God's grace opened my eyes to focus on His plan for my life.

*Romans 5:1-21 ESV*
*Therefore, since we have been justified by faith, we have peace with God through our Lord Jesus Christ. Through him we have also obtained access by faith into this grace in which we stand, and*

*we rejoice in hope of the glory of God. More than that, we rejoice in our sufferings, knowing that suffering produces endurance, and endurance produces character, and character produces hope, and hope does not put us to shame, because God's love has been poured into our hearts through the Holy Spirit who has been given to us.*

I have learned when you walk in your confidence it makes you more attractive. Words of support and encouragement at home help you know who you are and who God is calling you to be. I was blessed to receive many words of encouragement and guidance from my parents, aunties, uncles and grandparents.

How your parents speak of you, what they tell you, how you are treated among your siblings and what you believe to be true is important in shaping your confident image as a child of God.

Victoria Osteen tells the story of when she was a child she always knew "she was supposed to be special."

I too, know I am special in God's eyes. He has been showing me through dreams and visions of the life direction He wants me to take.

When I was nine years old the Lord put the fictional character Detective Doublahub into my mind. Doublahub could do anything; she solved crimes and was super smart. I don't know what inspired a nine year old to create this powerful young Detective. I was living in the 1970s at the time so there were lots of crime fighters out there on TV just not many women.

There was Sergeant Pepper Anderson, Police Woman. She was a role model for me even though she's a fictional character. I was blessed to meet Angie Dickinson the actress that played Pepper Anderson at a police conference. I was happy to share my story and enjoyed meeting her. Knowing who you are could influence the next generation to choose a profession like yours.

Being set apart and called to set an example has been part of my life since childhood. I always knew people were watching me.

As my family traveled with my father's work we were always the new kids in town. Often times we were the only black children in town. Being raised as a Catholic, I knew I had to be on my best behavior. God was watching.

From the time I was a Girl Scout, to the time that I was in student leadership in high school, to the time that I was in student leadership in college, to the time that I was in the Reserve Officer Training Corps (ROTC) at the University I attended, to the time I got commissioned as a military officer, to the time that I became a police officer, to the time that I became a trainer of police, to the time I became a chaplain, to the time I became a trainer of chaplains, to the time I became a professional development speaker; I was always in the spotlight. Always being watched.

These were all positions of leadership in positions of integrity with expectations of behavior.

As a Christian, which is my highest calling, I know that God is always watching. I must do everything that I do for His glory.

I have been blessed to travel the world and speak as a minister, chaplain and as a Law Enforcement Officer. I've been able to share at Women's Conferences internationally. And all these positions I was front and center. I was on stage, which meant that God was on stage because His Holy Spirit is in me in everything I do and wherever I go.

*Matthew 5:16 NIV*
*Let your light so shine before men, that they may see your good works, and glorify your Father in Heaven.*

I encourage you to actively do things to affect and change the world for people, and addressing them causes that affect. Use your voice; speaking, traveling and training around the world. Use your platform, the titles, and positions of influence that you've been blessed with and realize that leadership has its privileges and it also has its responsibilities.

Know that if you are reading this chapter that you have a call on your life. We are called to lead. The most important person that we learn to lead is ourselves. We become our first mission. We must focus daily on being our best. What helps us focus? Be focused on Jesus and what he requires of us in our daily lives. We must make a point of supporting, celebrating and encouraging those that the Lord puts into our lives.

Is it just me, or have other people such as your mother or perhaps even a strong influencer in your life, told you "they are just jealous!" when you spoke of peers or naysayer who attempted to discourage you in your life pursuits and joys?

They say things like:

"You can't do that!"

"Who do you think you are?"

"That's stupid!"

"It won't work!"

"You won't get it!"

True or not, it was a strong statement which helped me realize that everyone is not on my side. Everyone will not understand my mission in life. Everyone is not my ally.

I've been told 20% of the people you meet or speak to during your life, whether in passing at the supermarket, or when you're speaking from the stage, will not like you.

That's not your concern. You cannot please everyone because they are coming from their own place with their own issues, perspectives and prejudice.

Pre-judging. This happens based on who they are and how they were raised. The decisions and thoughts they choose to embrace and actions at the moment.

Do not chase the 20%. Serve the 80% with your message

God's grace calls us to live our lives with purpose. God's purpose. How do we know our purpose? How do we know our mission?

We ask God for guidance. We pray and seek the Lord's direction. We dedicate each day to the Lord and check in daily and throughout the day to make sure we are on task. I speak more about daily intimacy with God in my chapter in our book "Faith Is Inspiring Stories from Las Vegas Chaplains"

*2 Corinthians 12:9 ESV*
*But he said to me, "My grace is sufficient for you, for my power is made perfect in weakness." Therefore I will boast all the more gladly of my weaknesses, so that the power of Christ may rest upon me.*

If we see Distractions and Temptations coming our way we resist them and flee from them. If we are unable to flee due to our sinful nature, which often influences us to stumble, we immediately pray, ask for forgiveness and repentance while re-setting ourselves on the right path.

The Lord is faithful and just to forgive us.
Look into your heart and see the passion that God has placed in you.

Are you a righter of wrongs?

Do you enjoy doing things for others?

Do you like to connect with people one on one?

Do you like to build and repair and discover things?

Do you like to host people?

Do you like to solve problems?

I encourage you to use the skills you have right where you are. The Lord uses us where He has placed us and He lets us know the way by way of open doors or closed ones. He speaks to some in dreams or through other people placed in your life. The Lord communicates with each of us in His own unique way.

Seek wise Godly counsel for confirmation that you're hearing from God in your desires and chosen path. Ensure you are surrounded by strong people of faith who can pray with you and also give insight into your decisions which help reference you're calling and purpose. Let them know what you are looking to pursue. Who you choose to fellowship with can affect your ability to serve God, and to properly walk in your purpose.

Consider the story of the Eagle and the chicken. Eagles soar above in a position where they can see all that's going on above, around, and beneath them. Chickens sadly have been known to peck at the ground and each other, eating worms or substance given to them by a caretaker. Chickens don't often look up; chickens hang in clusters and cluck. We know people who fit this description in all professions.

To learn to fly or soar above the chickens, the chicken must look up and seek out Eagles and watch what the Eagle does. He must then connect with the Eagle and ask the eagle how she learned to soar so high, and how he can too?

This of course is a visual story. It's rare that a chicken will fly and those which do cannot fly far. Most chickens don't know how to fly, and never attempt to fly. While looking down or across at eye level they do not see the sky? Do they even know that there is a place to soar up high in the sky?

Don't be a chicken.

Look up.

Look up to Jesus.

He's calling us all to More.

He's calling us to look at eternity and know we are building our treasures in heaven by what we do while here on earth.

He's calling us to prepare and bring others with us.

He's calling us to be vigilant and aware of how we can be of service.

I am an Eagle. Called to Lead Eagles. Called to fly amongst the Eagles and to see the Big Picture, to serve God, His mission and my fellow man.

What is your Call?

*Acts 20:24 ESV*
*But I do not account my life of any value nor as precious to myself, if only I may finish my course and the ministry which I received from the Lord Jesus, to testify to the gospel of the grace of God.*

So be thankful for God's grace and all He has seen you through and seek to continue walking in your God planned mission.

# Senior Chaplain Victorya

Victoria is a Nevada State licensed Minister Officiate

She is the Founder and Executor Director of Messages of Faith Ministry and its Chaplaincy division, with approximately 300 Chaplains serving the Southern Nevada area. She is published, and the Christian author of, *Chosen 15 Minutes with Jesus, and *Born Again.

She has co-sponsored with educational entities in S. Nevada for over 20 yrs., i.e. UNLV EO. She holds a 4th degree Black Belt in TKD, and was a Tournament Certified Referee for 8 years under Grand Master D.S. Kim. In 2015 she was awarded the Lifetime Achievement Recognition for her work from the NV State Governors Office, US Senatorial, US House of Representatives, US House of Congress, and from partnered community organizations. In 2018 she received the CLV Mayors Initiative RECAP Award. She is an Invocator for the CC Commissioners and CLV Mayor/ Council.

On January 21st 1998 she had a divine face to face encounter with Jesus Christ, His message was on forgiveness, His revelation was on God the Father. Her testimony aired on CBN Christian Broadcasting Network the700 Club and CBN 700 Club Interactive in July 2017 and in 2018. Victorya's message is, Jesus Is Alive and He wants us to forgive.

www.Victorya.net

†Chapter Two

# No Greater Love Than Jesus

*By SR Chaplain Victorya*

*There is therefore now no condemnation to them which are in Christ Jesus, who walk not after the flesh, but after the Spirit, Romans 8:1-39*

Love is, and can be present in many forms and come from different directions, sometimes it can move slowly while surprising us, and other times we don't even see it coming, meanwhile hitting us as some say, like a brick of cement. We have different forms of love such as family, friends, work, pets, art, sports, religions, etc., all coming from different directions which can create and develop numerous relationships and types of love.

The years, the relationships, have all taught me that real love comes from someone far greater than any earthly affection I had ever developed or believed in. There has only been one person in my life that taught me what real love is, and who real love comes from, and His name is Jesus. There has never been an experience in my life that encountered divine love such as that; which came from Jesus and being born again in Him, nor has anyone ever explained true love such as He did when He proclaimed "I am the Way, the

Truth, and the Life" and "Faith, Hope and Love, but the greatest of these is love". There is no greater love under heaven than Jesus.

I look back at all the different areas in life where I didn't see, or realize, or believe that anyone was watching over me, or standing with me, or cared what was or might be happening in my life that was causing me concern, or stress, hopelessness, or depression. When you feel you're standing on a battlefield alone defending yourself against all those who are waging war against you, when you feel like giving up and putting down your sword because the enemy's tiresome arrows fly by day and by night against you, and you cry out "where is God".

Then a revelation comes, and a peace flows through you that passes all understanding, when you gain the strength to stand up, and continue the good fight, you open your eyes and know that the love of Christ has mercifully and gracefully walked you through another storm in life, in love.

There are so many examples in my life of where the love of Jesus has shown His tenderness for me, that it's hard to pick just one sample as being a greater case of kindness than the next. Every wrongdoing I have committed in which I am thoroughly accountable for is wiped away by His blood and grace, healing my sorrow and repentant heart. Who does this? The love of Jesus does.

Many years ago when I was living in Southern California during a night of drinking and partying with friends the clock hit 2:00AM; which means lights out, closing up, and time to go home, except I wasn't ready to go home. I left with a friend and deciding to go to Tijuana where the clubs don't close at 2 AM. As we started on our way suddenly we saw the lights flashing behind us, so we pulled over. They arrested him for a warrant and left me sitting in the car.

I decided to drive over to one of my girlfriend's house to see if she was up however she wasn't home. Her brother and another friend were standing outside the house and we started talking about what had just occurred, and the fact that I was left with a car was all to inviting, so we decided the three of us would take a drive to Mexico and hang out for a couple of hours, unfortunately it wouldn't work out that way.

Once we reached Tijuana we decided we would rather continue on to Ensenada. Traveling down the road I looked up to see a highway sign with Ensenada and the mileage written but as soon as I noticed it I heard a voice from within revealing that an accident was about to happen, just then I heard the skidding of tires and the sound of screaming as my body was being tossed about and ultimately tossed from the vehicle.

I was staring into what looked to be a pond of dark water, and the water seemed to have ripples, then from deep within the ridge I saw a word forming that said "die" it began flowing within the crease of the water, then the word slowly transformed itself into "go back", thus again flowing within the ripple. I opened my eyes, I was in an ambulance and one of the EMTs was looking at me and he had his hand beneath my blouse, and then it was dark again.

I opened my eyes and tried to focus, everything was unfamiliar. I was lying on a table and I could hear voices, and then yelling and weeping. I rose up slowly from the table and made my way to the doorway, the voices were coming from behind it. I slowly opened the door and a man wearing a white jacket was standing directly in front of me, his body was blocking who he was speaking to but I knew it was my friends. I was stunned as I listened to what he was saying, he was telling them "she didn't make it", and I thought to myself who died, who is he referring to, and then it hit me, he was talking about me.

I began to panic trying to figure out why he would be telling them I died when clearly I hadn't. I closed the door and began looking around for another way out of the room, there was only one other door to the room and it led to a restroom. I looked at the small window as I climbed on top of the toilet hoping I would fit through it, I lifted myself up and climbed down the other side. I made my way around the building stepping slowly, my body ached and my head hurt, realizing they had stitched up my forehead as I could feel where the wound had been bandaged.

I made my way over to a window and cautiously peeked through it, I saw both my friends sitting there but the man in the white coat was nowhere to be seen. I tapped lightly on the window trying to get their attention; they finally looked up and were reacting as if they were looking at a ghost. Realizing it was really me they were seeing, they knew they had been lied to. I pointed to the room I had been in and told them I climbed out of the bathroom window, they hurried over to the room however only one of them made it out, the other one was arrested and it took his family weeks to have him released, the Mexico police cited road damages and made the family pay a hefty price.

One of them made it through the window and freed himself, that's when the yelling began and men inside the building began grabbing on to the other one, all I heard was "run". The two of us began running down the hill, it was the first time I noticed the building sat uphill in a wooded area, running we were ducking in and out of the trees. We could hear the sound of cars coming down the hill, so we stopped and sat on the ground behind one of the larger bushes, the cars kept going onward yet slowing down every few feet; we waited until they passed far enough down the hill and we began running again.

As we made it to the foot of the hill, a man in an old truck was coming down the road so we waved him down and asked for a ride to town. He was an older man and he sat there looking at me with my cuts, bruises and bandages as if he was deciding what to do, he finally nodded his head and motioned for us to get in.

Our driver not only took us into Tijuana but he drove us all the way to the border. From the American side of the border we hitchhiked all the way back home. Needless to say when I walked through the door my mother looked as if she might have a heart attack and immediately took me to the doctors. I received an earful that day. The years passed by and every so often I would be reminded of that experience, but I never understood the purpose of the lie, telling my friends I had died, and I had never heard any explanation offered.

Fast forward- years later I had started working in Ministry and becoming involved in some of the community and faith-based initiatives of problematic issues concerning youth and adults, gangs, human and sex trafficking, prison reform amongst other controversial topics. One day after reading an email on human/sex trafficking sent out by one of the local churches I decided to register for the event to learn more about it. I received my registration confirmation and when the date of the event rolled around I headed out the door to attend.

At the event I gathered up brochure materials available and seated myself at one of the tables near the stage. The forum of speakers began and video clips were being shown. As I sat there taking in all the information a woman began speaking of her personal story, she began explaining the sex trafficking business, I remember sitting there listening to her in complete disbelief and horror, and suddenly the sounds in the room became very faint, and then it was as if a bright light was turned on, and I heard His voice say "Do you see what I saved you from", and suddenly it was as if I was transmitted back in time, and my mind was on a re-run of the day of the accident in Mexico, and here once again I was listening to the Dr. say "I'm sorry she didn't make it".

"Do you see what I saved you from" I was stunned to my very core, what a foolish young girl I had been, never once in my life had I ever imagined the purpose of that lie, it was all a plan for kidnapping and trafficking, I had never even heard of that possibility back then. A young girl of eighteen in an accident in another country, a perfect plot, they didn't worry about returning the body of a dead girl they could have insisted she was already buried in that foreign land. Who would have been the wiser? My family would have fought to have me back, but my mother was single and living on a small income, she would never have been able to pay all the bureaucracy that would have been involved.

When we don't have all the information, when we are lost and confused, when there isn't an inkling to everything involved in the matter, when we think we are smarter than the average bear, and then God unfolds the truth before our very eyes and ears, we are humbled. I thought I knew it all, I thought I made it out of that situation based on my own instincts, but that couldn't have been further from the truth.

Every step from my first mistake of making the choice to take a car and travel out of my own country into another country, to not inform family of my whereabouts, deciding to continue to drink and party, all led me to being thrown from a car and landing half way down a cliff lying above the ocean floor, and available for one of the most evil trades in the world to have access to me. Who else but the love of Jesus could make a way, could shine a light, could be the guiding force, could disrupt and thwart the enemy, and could save me in such a way? Jesus was with me every step of the way, not because I deserved, and not because I earned, but because of His grace and mercy, and because of His love for me and His plan for my life.

Fast forward to 2018 I was invited to speak at an International Conference on Human/Sex Trafficking in Las Vegas; my topic was on "Professional Objectives listed from a faith-based perspective." When I concluded my portion of the conference I also gave the audience my Mexico testimony and experience including my eye-opening "Do you see what I saved you from" revelation from God.

Some of the subjects' topics and notes were given as follows;
*"Religious leaders and faith communities are making significant contributions and development, in the areas faith initiatives, social issues, community development, family issues, even extending into the political initiatives Strategies includes working with religious leaders to address both religious and non-religious causes of*

*violence and support their ongoing initiatives to build peaceful societies.*

*Non-governmental organizations and nonprofits have enlisted international, national and local religious groups in the fight against trafficking and prostitution of people. Many religions and its people of faith believe that fighting human trafficking is of a moral and religious imperative. Moral repair" is needed to undo the damage done by society, and faith based can be used in that unique role to help combat the broken compass of evil.*

*Churches and faith-based have first-hand knowledge of the pain caused by broken communities, which means the faith community can play an increasingly important role in helping to affect police and community trust. The faith based can serve as a critical link between government and law enforcement.*

*--Relationships between law enforcement and the faith community begin on building a personal trust. Government officials, Court Judges, and Police also worship in their local churches.*
*--Religious figures can serve as a powerful calming influence, and defusing potentially violent situations, they can help build the gap between law enforcement and the public.*
*--We all know that human trafficking is slavery in the modern age. Churches and faith-based organizations can help to raise awareness, and be a voice in the fight against trafficking. They can*

*educate themselves and others in recognizing, and assisting victims of trafficking.*

*With churches and faith-based communities working with local law enforcement agencies on a local level, this helps provide a larger spectrum for opening the slot, and helps to adopt more effective strategies against human trafficking on an international level."* Information and lecture notes were compiled from viable faith and government resources in combatting human/sex trafficking to include applicable faith-based and government statistics.

God will always confirm His Word; He will always confirm His revelation of Himself to us. What I thought was just one of those life-lessons turned out to be a lesson, repentance, forgiveness, and another molding of transformation in my life, the Lord leaves no work undone and He completes all of His work. There is no amount of instinct or knowledge in my life in which I claim pride in, but there is a vast volume of grace and mercy that cannot be contained or understood by man when it comes to the benevolence of Almighty God.

Love is Jesus, His love for humanity, the hedge of protection He wraps around all those who belong to Him in, it is undeniable. The world has never known a greater love than Jesus Christ, and I have never known a greater love than my Jesus. Love Is Jesus!

*We love him, because he first loved us 1 John 4:19*

# Senior Chaplain Barry Mainardi

Chaplain Barry graduated from the University of Dayton. He served with the U.S. Army as an Airborne Jumpmaster/Instructor Pilot and in two areas of combat including Vietnam. He received an Honorable Discharge at the rank of Captain.

Chaplain Barry is an Ordained Senior Chaplain with Chaplaincy Nevada, serving as Director of Administration and Past chair of the Advisory Board; Co-Chair of SNV Community Gang Task Force – Human Trafficking; 4 years as Las Vegas Mayor's Faith Based Initiative - Human Trafficking Co-Chair; RECAP (Rebuilding Every City Around Peace) First Responder; So. NV Human Trafficking Task Force (METRO) Education Committee; NV Coalition to Prevent the Commercial Sexual Exploitation of Children Committees; SNV-VOAD (SNV Volunteers Active in Disaster) Board member; CLV Master Plan Citizens Advisory Committee; and serves as a Las Vegas METRO Volunteer. Barry is a certified Maxwell EQUIP Course Instructor and serves as an Arbitrator for the Financial Industries Regulatory Authority.

†Chapter Three

# Love Is Unconditional

*By SR Chaplain Barry Mainardi*

I attended a class recently and the instructor asked us to describe God's Love. My response was almost immediate because I thought the answer was obvious to me … so I responded:

"God is love because we are so imperfect, make so many mistakes, sin constantly, always ask for forgiveness, sin again and He still takes us back. Only a Perfect Being could love so many imperfect people. He demonstrates His love by choosing us to do His work. His only requirement is our acknowledgment that we believe in Him. He knew us before we were born; as written in Jeremiah 1:5 (NIV): Before I formed you in the womb I knew you, before you were born I set you apart; I appointed you as a prophet to the nations.'"

Therefore, He knows what we will do during our lives and still chooses us for His Glory. Jesus knew His Love for The Father while on the cross when He asked why He had been forsaken. Jesus meant, He did not want to be away from God's Love for a moment even though it was ordained that this would happen because it was essential to our salvation. Matthew 27:46 (NIV) clearly emphasized this:

"About three in the afternoon Jesus cried out in a loud voice, "Eli, Eli, lema sabachthani?" (which means "My God, my God, why have you forsaken me?")

But then I asked myself; what about forgiveness?

What about judging the actions of others and holding them accountable?

What about the Confidence/Trust we placed in others who ultimately betrayed us?

I know we all have these questions because we face challenges every day. So, let's begin by discussing "What is Love". As I see it, Love is Unconditional and requires:

Sacrifice

Sincere actions on our part

Finally, Our Lord Commands us to Love one another

There are many scriptures that discuss and reinforce our Lord's Command that we love each other.

 John 13:34-35 is a powerful message:

34 "A new command I give you: Love one another. As I have loved you, so you must love one another. 35 By this everyone will know that you are my disciples, if you love one another."

I am sure some of you noticed that I stated, "Finally, Our Lord Commands us to Love one another". This was placed LAST on the list when some of you may think it should be first. Well, perhaps we should think of His "Command" in a different manner.

I believe we should obey God's Commands because we love Him. John 14:21 tells us:

"Whoever has my commands and keeps them is the one who loves me. The one who loves me will be loved by my Father, and I too will love them and show myself to them."

Need more evidence? The Lord knows what is in our hearts and I feel if we "love" others because He commands us, we are not truly and unconditionally loving, we conditionally love because of fear. John told us in 1 John 4:18:

"There is no fear in love. But perfect love drives out fear, because fear has to do with punishment. The one who fears is not made perfect in love."

So, I pray we agree that our Lord loves us unconditionally and I pray we Love Him unconditionally primarily because that is our desire. But, what about loving all these imperfect humans (like you and me), some of whom are "wolves in sheep clothing"? Are we supposed to love them unconditionally also?

Let us begin by defining "unconditional love" ... The Urban Dictionary defines unconditional love as "affection without any limitations or love without conditions. This term is sometimes associated with other terms such as true altruism or complete love".

34

Our Lord did not command us to love conditionally under the following situations or actions, He said, "… You must love each other …". However, even though our Lord expects us to love unconditionally, to say "YES" to Him lovingly is a better way to show our Lord that we Revere Him and not just Fear Him.

Unconditional Love and Forgiveness
Unconditional Love and Forgiveness act as "partners" helping us get closer to our Lord. Loving unconditionally allows us to forgive immediately but if we have difficulty obeying His Command, forgiving others guides us to love unconditionally.

Let us begin by discussing the importance of Forgiveness: Forgiveness is an essential part of unconditional love because forgiveness releases us as well as those who hurt us. Forgiveness allows us to "move on" from the trauma or event so we are able to focus on His Path, not our emotions. We all believe that we must forgive, but because we are human, sometimes we have to forgive many times until … we actually are successful forgiving someone. Even Peter had difficulty forgiving his enemy. As Matthew says in 18:21-22:
"Then Peter came up and said to him, "Lord, how often will my brother sin against me, and I forgive him? As many as seven times?" Jesus said to him, "I do not say to you seven times, but seventy-seven times.""

I have many experiences where forgiveness allowed me to love unconditionally. But a recent challenge comes to mind.

Someone with whom I associate betrayed me and it could have interfered with my mission. My feelings for his actions were more flesh than Spirit, so I decided to ignore him. My attitude created an environment where his eyes lower every time our paths crossed but I also noticed an uncomfortable feeling within me. One day, the Spirit told me it was my responsibility to "make things right". An opportunity presented itself where I complimented him on a successful project in which he participated. Our relationship noticeably improved. Now there is peace in his eyes when we interact, and I feel I am at peace which allows me to follow His path as He intended and not through my flesh.

We are all imperfect:

We must agree that we are all imperfect and make mistakes. Most of our mistakes are unintentional because we did not wait on the Lord before we acted, and some are intentional ... which means our flesh blocked our view of the Holy Spirit when we acted. Loving unconditionally requires dedicated effort on our part and it does not come naturally because our flesh gets in the way. The devil will try to convince us that someone does not deserve our love. When that happens, we should us what Paul tells us in Corinthians 13:4-7 as a checklist:

"4 Love is patient, love is kind. It does not envy, it does not boast, it is not proud. 5 It does not dishonor others, it is not self-seeking, it is not easily angered, it keeps no record of wrongs. 6 Love does not delight in evil but rejoices with the truth. 7 It always protects, always trusts, always hopes, and always perseveres."

Unconditional Love means regardless of the actions or consequences, loving everyone must be the foundation of how we live our lives.

Righteous Judgment & Accountability is our duty

I believe Righteous Judgment and holding ourselves Accountable are responsibilities assigned by God and require our attention. Before I discuss these important responsibilities, it is important for us to realize that these responsibilities can only be achieved successfully if we love unconditionally.

As soon as we accept these responsibilities, we must allow the Holy Spirit to guide us, so we remember; we are righteously judging and holding others accountable to bring us all closer to God. If we allow our flesh to intervene, our results will be harmful to both those in question and ourselves.

I will admit there are times when it is not easy to love unconditionally. The actions of others that result in hurting others such as sexual exploitation of children, domestic violence, injustice, slander, and greed are just a few demonic actions that test our belief that we should love everyone. It is important that we exclude these challenges from loving unconditionally but use them as guidelines when deciding with whom we associate, work or form relationships.

I believe it will be easier for us if we understand without "Love", these responsibilities will inhibit our desire to obey Him.

Remember, we are imperfect, so we can use all the help we can get. We must always ask ourselves, "Do I allow these my flesh to block my ability to love unconditionally"?

The Bible says we are supposed to judge others, but we are to do so righteously, not by being self-serving. How else are we able to help others? Aren't we supposed to correct someone who has strayed from the path the Lord set? Of course we are, and there are many scriptures that support my belief such as John 7:24, which states: "Do not judge by appearances, but judge with right judgment."

… and Paul who wrote in Galatians 6:1:

"Brothers, if anyone is caught in any transgression, you who are spiritual should restore him in a spirit of gentleness. Keep watch on yourself, lest you too be tempted."

Holding each other Accountable is an integral part of righteous judging. We are ultimately accountable for our thoughts and our actions to God. Matthew 12:36-37 reminds us that God determines Accountability, not us:

"But I tell you that every careless word that people speak, they shall give an accounting for it in the day of judgment. "For by your words you will be justified, and by your words you will be condemned."

However, we are placed here to be trained and grow in the Lord. We have a responsibility to bring others closer to our Lord and holding each other accountable is a means to that end. Proverbs 27:17 & 27 tell us:

"17 Iron sharpens iron, and one man sharpens another; 23Know well the condition of your flocks, And pay attention to your herds"

I am blessed to serve on several panels in which we determine "accountability" for actions that are being questioned. If I do not love unconditionally, it is not possible for me to judge accountability righteously. The same accountability standard applies to family, friends and associates. We must hold each other accountable because we love them, or we will be judged as we judge.

Confidence/trust in others:

There is difference between "Complete Trust" and "Confidence/trust in others". We commonly use the term, "trust", when referring to someone upon whom we depend during our partnerships or relationships while we are "here-on-earth". Let me clarify the difference:

Complete Trust is reserved for the Lord. Never place our complete trust in "man", who is imperfect. Once we base our trust in "man", we will begin to negate the trust we must have in our Lord. Jeremiah 17:7-8 is one of many scriptures that tell us why:

7 "Blessed is the man who trusts in the Lord, whose trust is the Lord, 8 He is like a tree planted by water, that sends out its roots by

the stream, and does not fear when heat comes, for its leaves remain green, and is not anxious in the year of drought, for it does not cease to bear fruit."

Confidence/trust in those with whom we associate is the positive feeling we have on someone's ability, qualities or ideas, based on our experience with that person. We call that "trust" but it is limited by the imperfections of "man". There will be times when our confidence/trust in someone will fail because of negative actions.

Proverbs 25:19 tells us: "Putting confidence in an unreliable person is like chewing with a toothache or walking on a broken foot." We live on earth with imperfections all around us, but we must depend on each other to do His Work. In order to do that, we must have confidence in those with whom we associate and depend on their performance.

Unfortunately, sometimes our confidence in someone is misplaced. The result may be a feeling of being betrayed, disappointed and possibly overwhelmed. Simply stated, place Complete Trust in our Lord and Confidence/trust in "man". However, there is Good News, as Romans 8:28 promises us:
"And we know that in all things God works for the good of those who love him, who have been called according to his purpose."

I remember many experiences when betrayal resulted in pain, whether it was divorce, workplace environment, friendships or relationships. But without those experiences, I would not be here today serving the Lord. Think about your prior pain. For those who Believe, our pain is healed because the Lord opened doors for us and we are able to use those experiences to help others.

## HOW DOES THIS HELP ME?

We are challenged every day but there are times when our flesh tells us not to Love Unconditional and Forgive others. When that happens, we must remember, we are all human and imperfect. We also must understand that Satan will attempt to use our imperfections against us as he tries to divert our path from the one set for us by our Lord. He will attack during our weaknesses, anger, frustration, guilt, denial and other human frailties to which we are susceptible. In short, we will always fall short of His Glory but we must trust that our Lord will be there for us no matter what we experience.

As Paul explained in Romans 3:23-34:

23 for all have sinned and fall short of the glory of God, 24 and all are justified freely by his grace through the redemption that came by Christ Jesus.

How would we feel if our Lord did not love us unconditionally because we sin, ask for forgiveness and sin again? He Loves us Unconditionally in spite of our imperfections.

41

The Bible states we are made in the image of God. That means God's character is reflected in us. This is represented in both the Old Testament and New Testament:

Genesis 1:26-27 states "God created man in His own image, in the image of God He created him; male and female He created them".

1 Corinthians 15:49 reinforces our image by telling us "49 And just as we have borne the image of the earthly man, so shall we bear the image of the heavenly man".

This means even with our imperfections, we are meant to follow His Image and act accordingly. Obviously, Satan cannot defeat God, but he can certainly try to use our imperfections against us.

THOUGHTS TO TAKE WITH YOU

Unconditional Love is commanded by The Father and how Jesus lived. We were created His image. If we cannot love those on earth unconditionally, then how can we love God unconditionally? Unconditional Love allows us to forgive others because forgiveness benefits those who forgive as much as those who are forgiven. Forgiveness allows us to go forward in His footsteps … Unconditionally.

Unconditional Love allows us to Judge Righteously and holds each other Accountable to bring us all closer to God, not to "get even". We should all Pray for the strength and courage to Love Unconditionally by the Spirit and not conditionally by the flesh.
Remember, Jesus is watching!

# Senior Chaplain Karen R. Atlantic

*May God's grace, peace and love, deliver, heal, and set free! Chaplain Karen*

Karen is not shy when sharing the Gospel of Jesus Christ or in teaching practical application, principals, and percepts of the Word of God. Karen has a heart to serve the homeless, the incarcerated, down trodden, the abused; children, and those who feel the affliction of hopelessness.

Being transparent, she openly shares her walk with God and the lessons learned in all her short comings she refers to as her "dirty" in a relatable manner in hope to "…become all things to all people so that by all possible means I might save some…" Corinthians 9:22 NIV

Karen. R. Atlantic, BS, MS, is currently employed with Clark County Department of Family Services. Karen earned her Masters of Science Degree in Psychology and Community Counseling from Troy State University, Alabama. Karen's greatest and most rewarding position is to serve God and the object of His love…people.

†Chapter Four

Love Is What My Father Taught Me

*By SR Chaplain Karen R. Atlantic*

It was 1984, Fulda, Germany, Downs Barracks Chapel. What a beautiful Sunday morning to celebrate Fathers' Day. As I watched the dads of our military community's children celebrate their dads; as parents celebrated their dads and their grandfathers, I realized that I could not relate to what was happening around me. As the choir began to sing "My Father's House", I became bewildered and sadden. A rush of emotions suddenly arose causing me inner turmoil and as quickly as the internal storm began, I closed my eyes and held my breath as I saw her standing in the entrance of the apartment, using her body to brace herself against the cold metal frame of the doorway; her arms spread wide with one arm holding the door open; one leg lifted waist high crying while her other leg anchored her body within the frame of the door.

He was standing in front of her; towering over her 5'3 frame staring at her not saying a word. She turned to her left to see her 4 small children, 2 boys and 2 girls, staring in silence at the scene before their eyes. The silence broke in the apartment when the woman screamed "Go to Miss Ann's house. Tell her to call the police!" I saw one of the little girls run under the woman's leg, into the outer hallway that led to additional apartments. She counted "1, 2, 3-Miss Ann's house".

The little girl returned to her own apartment. Mission accomplished. The woman closed the front door to the apartment after the little girl returned. The woman told all the children to go back to bed as she walked into the living room and sat in the orange chair that was in the middle of the hallway having a clear view of the front door, the children's bedrooms and the kitchen entrance. The man was sitting on a chair in the kitchen at the table. The man is the little girl's dad. As the little girl walked towards her bedroom that she shared with her sister, she went into the kitchen. She glanced at the kitchen window and saw that it was still night-time as she walked up to the man and said, "I'm sorry daddy." He responded: "That's ok." I am that little girl. That was the year I was in kindergarten. I was 4 years old. I could hear the choir sing the verse:
"Lay aside every weight that so easily besets you, step out on your faith, my Father wants to bless you. Take your troubles and all your cares to the Lord and leave them there. Come and go with me to my Father's house…"

In what seemed to be a still framed moment in time, in an instant, for the first time the emotions I experienced were connected to the flash-back that I had had many countless days while awake and sleepless nights. What seemed like an hour had passed; it was actually a second or two. I began to cry aloud. Hot tears coupled with soft screams of anguish. No one really noticed me. It was a Gospel Service and the parishioners were worshipping God; singing with the choir, and dancing in the Spirit. The Holy Spirit began to minister to me. Then I heard: "I have not abandoned you. I love you with an everlasting love. I have always been with you, protected you, and provided for you. You are not an orphan. You are my beloved child and I am your Father." That was the day Father God became my "Daddy-God". As the choir sang the chorus:

"Come and go with me to my Father's house. Come and dine at His table and rest there. Then find joy and peace, love and happiness; come and go with me to my Father's house."

The Holy Spirit continued to show me how the next 6 years preceding that one night, changed the trajectory of the lives of my family forever.

I was in the 6th grade when it happened. I remembered my mom telling me and my siblings, "Daddy doesn't live here anymore". My parents had separated. One day I came home from school and after settling in, preparing to do my homework, I heard a knock at the door. My mom was in the kitchen hanging curtains. I answered the door by asking "who is it?" the voice replied, "It's you father". I opened the door and let him in. He walked into the kitchen where my mom was. As I sat in the living room, I could hear his voice through the cinder block painted wall, but I could not understand what he was saying. Mommy called me into the kitchen and said,

"Go to Miss Chase's house and ask her if I could borrow a light bulb". I glanced at him. He was sitting at the kitchen table. Off to the 6th floor I went. Miss Chase was not at home. I went back downstairs to the 4th floor to our apartment only to find the door wide opened. Panic churned away at my stomach. The apartment was empty.

I walked slowly into the apartment, into the kitchen. I could hear a commotion outside, so I looked outside from the kitchen window that faced the front of our apartment building to see my mom walking in circles holding her hand to her face. Blood was pouring out! I ran down 4 flights of stairs straight to my mom whose face and the front of her soft gray and white polka dot top was covered in blood, streaming down the front of her gray pencil skirt, down her the front of her legs, down to her bare feet,, making a puddle on the ground where she stood. The next sound I heard that drowned out the sound of her screaming voice was the ambulance and … police cars.

It was then that I realized my sister and brothers were home from school. We walked up the stairs together, following our older brother. My older brother asked me what happened. I told him that daddy came to see us, so I let him in and then mommy told me to go to Miss Chase's house to borrow a light bulb. My brother said, "How stupid are you!!? Really? Daddy took the hammer and hit mommy in her eye. He knocked her eyeball into the back of her head!" I began to cry as we continued to walk up the stairs.

We were directed to go to Miss Dottie's house by some adults who stopped us on the stairs. Miss Dottie lived on the 8th floor. I cried, and cried. My brother told me to shut up and if I had not let "him" in, mommy would be alright. I stopped crying just as we reached the 8th floor. That was the last time that I remembered crying uncontrollably, fervently and with abandonment. I could hear the choir sing the 2nd verse:

"If you're weary and need to be at rest, I hear Jesus say 'come lay upon my breast, for my yoke is easy and my burdens light; come and go with me to my Father's house…"

It was then I understood that although I had long since forgiven my dad and my brother, I had not been healed of the psychological and emotional hurt that had impacted my life from young childhood. Not knowing or understanding how family dynamics shape a child's belief system and how they engage with others; not understanding what a healthy relationship between a husband, wife and children ought to be and or how to mirror the relationships and their differences in a manner conducive to children. I had never considered that I needed to be healed.

I compared my pain to the pain that my mom must have suffered at the hands of my dad. She suffered more physical, mental and emotional pain than I would ever know by way of experience, or so I thought. I had not known that I had bouts of Posttraumatic Stress Syndrome as a result of living in a home characterized by severe domestic violence. My childhood past was hanging over me like a heavy cloud. The Holy Spirit prompted me to know that I have a mansion that has many rooms.

In my Father's house are many mansions: if it were not so, I would have told you. I go to prepare a place for you. John 14:2 King James Version (KJV)

Then I heard the choir sing the bridge:

"There are many mansions there, a land of cloudless day, where my loved ones wait for me; they're waiting at heaven's gate."

Rooms large enough and well equipped to eradicate the pains of my childhood past, present and future. In my Father's house I am being taught what love is. Love is not what my daddy showed me. Love is GOD and God is love. Love is not limited or conditional. Love heals me, makes me free from the hurt of my past; releases me from all guilt, all shame, all self-loathing, and the inability to forgive myself. I can take all traumatic experiences to the Father who has given me a crown of beauty instead of ashes, the oil of joy instead of mourning, and a garment of praise instead of a spirit of despair.

I am called an oak of righteousness, a planting of the LORD for the display of his splendor! Isaiah 61:3

I stood up from the pew where I have been sitting for about 6 minutes. As the choir sang the vamp, I clapped, danced, sang and shouted as steamy tears escaped from my eyes in total abandonment:

"Joy in the house. Love in the house. Peace in the house. Deliverance in the house. Salvation in the house. Healing in the house. Forgiveness in the house. Come and go with me to my Father's house, to my Father's house."

It is unknown to me or my siblings if there were any legal consequences for my dad's brutal actions. Why? He disappeared for several years. Today my dad resides with his wife of over 20 years. He refuses to talk about "the past". My mother was later diagnosed with Schizophrenia due to head trauma. My mom lived several years homeless. There was a period of time I did not know where she was. When I found her, she was residing in an adult group home for residents who had severe mental health diagnosis. My mother died on 08/07/2012, alone in her bedroom. At the time of her death, she was survived by 3 children, 4 grandchildren and 7 great grandchildren.

My older brother had lived a double life. A math whiz, who committed fraud again his employer and later completed his jail sentence for his crimes. His lifestyle was characterized by the abuse of my dad that he later disclosed to me that he suffered. I was in my 20's when my brother told me our dad was his dad. I later asked my dad if he was my brother's dad. My dad responded: "No, I'm not. I thought your mother told you." I remembered seeing my brother's birth certificate. His last name was the same as mine. My dad explained, "Back then, you could give a baby any name you wanted. There were no questions asked. I never had to adopt him."

My brother passed away in a hospital in North Carolina on 12/19/2008, due to diabetes complications.

My youngest brother resides in another State still dealing with the pain of his childhood past that has shaped him into the man he is today. My dear sister…it was never disclosed to me by my siblings, her only child or dad, that my sister had bizarre behaviors. I discovered this on my own when she called me to pick her up from the airport here in Las Vegas. She had decided to relocate from New Jersey. I had only understood that she would be coming to visit. After 4 months residing in my home, she disappeared. More than 2 years passed before Sunrise Hospital contacted me to inform that my sister was in the hospital in critical condition. During my days and nights spent with my sister, the anguish of not knowing where she was among the homeless population in Las Vegas which is unimaginable! I sang to her, praised God for her, she was a practicing Born Again Believer! I went through her belongings and found documentation from a mental health clinic with her diagnosis. I began to recall her account of the things she had suffered as a child and as an adult.

She chased after a love that she could only receive from a Heavenly Father who was waiting to heal her of her childhood pain that followed her through her adult life. Although she was on a respirator, she could hear me and respond by blinking and by squeezing my hand. We prayed for her healing of all the things that had her bound. The radiance upon her face is indescribable. I asked her if she was ready to "go home". She blinked and squeezed my hand. She did not die alone. I was there day and night until her passing. My sister closed her eyes on 05/04/2015 at 5:25pm and opened them to see the glory of the LORD!

I take comfort in knowing that my parents, siblings and a few other family members were the first ones that I shared the Gospel of Jesus Christ with upon my return to the United States from Germany, where the Lord Jesus met me where I was, caught in a bottomless pit of anguish and despair. He delivered me out of the clutches of the enemy. With great joy and excitement, I had to tell them…yes initially my siblings thought I had lost my mind, but they soon understood and committed their lives to the Lord. I trust God and His faithfulness to His Word that Mommy, Bryan, and Brenda now experience freedom and the ultimate love that pours out from my Father's heart, washing away every pain and every tear shown in anguish turned into sheer joy. "My hope is built on nothing less than Jesus' blood and righteousness!"

I take courage in writing the stories of my childhood and in knowing that there are more that must be told in hope that some will be healed, others will be delivered and set free by Love is…and is everlasting. I was made free from my childhood past.

My Father taught me that Love is…3 fold: Love the Lord your God with all your heart, mind and soul; secondly love your neighbor, and thirdly, as yourself… yourself… yourself! Love is not only an action word, a verb, it is also a choice. When you do not know what real love is, you have a Father too who is standing with arms wide open to welcome you regardless of how broken you are or what has caused your brokenness or who caused it. I rejoice in your discovery of what love is…

Are you tired? Worn out? Burned out on religion? Come to me. Get away with me and you'll recover your life. I'll show you how to take a real rest. Walk with me and work with me—watch how I do it. Learn the unforced rhythms of grace. I won't lay anything heavy or ill-fitting on you. Keep company with me and you'll learn to live freely and lightly."

Matthew 11:28-30 the Message (MSG)

# Senior Chaplain Walter Poston

Apostle Walter L. Poston is the Senior Pastor of Highways & Hedges Outreach Ministries along with his wife Pastor Pamela Poston. They are Chicago natives; with two grown children and three grandchildren.

He is a Senior Chaplain with Messages of Faith Ministries in Las Vegas. Apostle Poston attended Bible College and completed Biblical Studies while serving his country in the U.S. Armed Forces - 564 Military Police Company in Butzbach, Germany. After returning to the United States, Poston joined St. John COGIC, where he was trained for outreach ministry.

He was also trained through Prison Fellowship Ministry. He has ministered in Chicago, Texas, and Nevada State and County jails and prisons.

Professionally, Walter Poston was employed and certified as a Pharmaceutical Technician and is currently serving his community as an Outreach Specialist, Case Manager and Court Advocate for homeless individuals and families.

# Chapter Five

# Love Is a Healing Power

*By SR Chaplain Walter L. Poston*

There are many people who are seeking to be loved. They are searching for it in people, places, and things. Individuals believe, if they could only find the perfect companion; live in a good community, give birth to children, or have a successful career; life would serve them love on a golden platter.

What is love; where does it come from? Is it an emotion or deep feeling? These are questions to ponder. The goal of this chapter is to answer questions regarding true love and what it looks like in the process of healing. There must be something and/or someone greater than us, who can take the broken pieces of a shattered life and make us whole.

Hopelessness has flooded the United States like a river that has crossed it borders. Death and destruction have stretched forth their hands to steal, kill, and destroy anything that has to do with love, human life, relationships, family structure, and community. Our country is in danger of losing a generation to pain and sexual abuse. This epidemic has stolen many innocent lives and thrust them into dark places. Those individuals are now involved with drugs, alcohol, strip clubs, prostitution, human trafficking, crime, incarceration, abusive relationships, abortion, and worst of all suicide. How can this destruction be stopped, with hope provided for the hopeless? This evil has infiltrated the very core of a nation that was founded on Godly values and turned it into a Den of Thieves.

Warning to Parents:

On November 12, 2018, The Doctors TV Show aired; Clinical psychologist and attorney Dr. Lisa Strohman who shared frightening information about apps that could be putting our children at risk.

*1. Vault Apps*

*These vault or "calculator" apps are downloaded by kids to keep their digital lives private. These apps are often disguised as calculators and if someone/parent without the password tries to unlock it, the app may even take a photo of them. Yes, it will notify your child about your snooping! Dr. Strohman shares the startling statistics that the average age of children viewing pornography is 8 years old and chronic viewing is 11 years old.*

*2. Live Streaming Apps*

*These apps allow kids and teens to press one button and then record themselves live for the world! There is a new part of these apps which gives digital currency to children. This currency can then be converted to real money in PayPal. What are they doing to earn this money? Well, you can only imagine… Dr. Strohman* describes it as *"a digital strip platform for kids to make money!"* OB/GYN Dr. Nita Landry points out this is likely being funded by the person who want the kid to do certain tasks so a lot of times it's some type of predator who has the financial means to pay these kids."

## 3. Avatar Apps

On these digital platforms, kids can create their avatars to be characters representative of themselves. While it's fun, especially for kids who are a bit shy or awkward in real life, there is some danger in geo-gamification (online technique to encourage engagement). This allows the app to locate your child and those around him. Random strangers pop up nearby in avatar form, which opens the door for potential pedophiles disguised as avatars to meet children.

Dr. Strohman advises parents to understand what is on their children's phones. She advises parents to lock down their kid's phones when they first get them, so they don't have the ability to download anything without permission first. If your kids already have a phone, start fresh by going through every app they have with them.

Dr. Strohman says her policy with her children is she takes 24 hours to first review an app and then will discuss it with them. If possible, wait until your children are in high school to give them smartphones.

Personal Testimonies:

According to a female student at the University of Pittsburg, who dined with a fellow male classmate then visited his friend home for a drink. The next day she woke up undressed, and no recollection of what happened. Weeks later the young man made a comment about wanting to see her again and do what he did before. In the years since, she hasn't dwelled on the incident. She said, "It hasn't severely impacted her." "He's gone about his life, and I've gone about mine."

A male student at a University in North Carolina recalled a woman took advantage of him twice when he was intoxicated. The woman was a friend of a friend. While he was partying on his 21st birthday, he said, "She pulled me into her room and had sex with me." She did it again after he had gone bar-hopping on St. Patrick's Day. He said: "It was sexual assault both times, but I didn't press any charges against her."

A female student at the University of Michigan reported; she was flirting with a guy at a fraternity party, getting drunk on cheap vodka, when he invited her upstairs to his room. They started making out. The 19-year-old student remembers that much. She later woke up on a couch downstairs, not knowing what happened. She didn't report it to the authorities, due to fear of exposing what happened at the party.

There are countless individuals that have similar experiences. If this is your testimony, I encourage you to receive the saving grace of the Lord and go through the process of healing. Don't deny the abuse happened; embrace the healing power of God's Love.

My Truth:

My innocence was stolen; I was thrust into a dark place around 8-year-old. For the next 12 plus years, I had identity struggles with who I had become. The pain and shame of this sin was so great, it incarcerated my life; the demons took control of my soul!

When the sexual abuse first happened, I felt confused and ashamed of what was done to my young body. I remember the day it happened. The sun was shining; the sky was blue. It was a beautiful day, until I was called into a bedroom and forced to have sex with one of my female cousins; while another cousin watched. I carried this dark secret for many years. "Why did she take advantage of me?" I was only a child.

My detailed testimony of molestation is penned in the Faith Is book. On June 25, 1978, I prayed the prayer of repentance (see 2 Peter 3:9), and the evil spirits departed from my body. The transformation of my life was due the power of God's love. According to John 8:36, Christ has set me free!

Why do bad things happen to good people? This will be addressed in my upcoming manuscripts.

True Love:

Loving God is likened unto a man who chooses to marry his high school sweetheart. They first become friends, and then commit to a relationship with one another. Love is a commitment to give from the heart. Once this is established, the couple should move forward with marriage counseling; then getting married. The couple then confesses their marriage vows to one another to make this their life-long commitment. Our relationship with God must be based on love, faith, mercy, and grace. We must choose to love God with our whole heart and share His love with others. These godly characteristics should be demonstrated and proven in our lives (see James 4:7,10 and John 15:13).

"God is love, and everyone that loves is born of God" (1 John 4:7).

Forgiveness is Love:

The love of God in Christ is the foundation for forgiveness. Forgiveness could be difficult and painful to do in many situations, because the abuser maybe someone close to abused. If you are seeking freedom, you MUST forgive those who violated you. If you do what Jesus commanded, the blessings of the Lord will make you whole. The apostle Paul wrote: "God sanctifying you to become whole" (see 1Thessalonians 5:23).

Forgiving others of the sin they committed against you is an outward demonstration of God's love at work in you. The love of God will give you the strength to work through the pain and accomplish what Jesus instructed us to do. Jesus taught the people saying: "When you are praying, first forgive anyone you are holding a grudge against, so that your Father in heaven will forgive your sins, too. But if you do not forgive, neither will your Father which is in heaven forgive your sins" (Mark 11:25-26).

The salvation and sanctifying process of the spirit and soul is a powerful act of God. God will save, heal, and deliver us from the destruction of evil. What the devil meant for evil, God will made it good.

Let's look at the spirit and soul as it relates to God's healing virtue: "The LORD God formed man from the dust of the ground and breathed into his nostrils the breath of life; and man became a living soul" (Genesis 2:7). The soul is the personality, mind, emotions, and will of humans. The spirit is our identity. This is where Christ and evil desires dwell. When the apostle Paul wrote about God sanctifying us wholly; he was explaining how Jesus is faithful to cleanse the spirit and soul and preserve the body faultless until He returns to earth.

The soul is where the personality, conscious mind (thinking, reasoning), subconscious mind (belief system, attitudes), will (choices), emotions (feelings) dwell and operates. The soul is where satan tempts individuals to follow his evil arrangements and reject God.

The human spirit of individuals is where God, His Son Jesus Christ and the Holy Spirit dwells. Through Jesus, we have access into

God's glorious grace. Therefore, God fills us with the Spirit of wisdom and revelation, in the knowledge of Him (see Ephesians 1:17).

The devil cannot overcome the power of God in us. However, he fights for the possession of the soul (see Luke 4:1-13).
The violation of sexual sins produces unhealthy roots of rejection in the soul. This could cause mental illness, and/or dysfunctional behaviors. Therefore, forgiveness is a major component in the healing process. How can anyone be healed without receiving forgiveness of their own sins first. "For all have sinned and come short of the glory of God". (Romans 3:23) Forgiving the individual(s) of the sin that was committed against you, is a test of your faith in God. Forgiving the predator, will FREE you from the power of the abuse and abuser.  Jesus said: "Pray for them that despitefully used you". This is God's way of breaking the chains of darkness and severing any generational curses that may be in your family bloodline.

Along with forgiveness, confession of faith, prayer and fasting, and fellowshipping with Christ and His church should be part of your spiritual diet. If you live in the Spirit, your life will be filled with the glory of God. Just know as you experience healing, the powers of darkness will fight against your purpose
(see Ephesians 6:10-18).

Confession of Faith:

Find faith scriptures in the bible that speak to who God said you are. Start reading them out loud (see Proverbs 8:21). Take ownership of confessing scriptures. You need to hear yourself speaking God's Word. This will increase your faith and cleanse you of all filthiness of your spirit and soul. This is the Lord consecrating you unto Himself. Here are a few faith scriptures: 2 Corinthians 5:17, Romans 8:1-4,14-17, 24,25, Acts 1:8, Jeremiah 29:1, and John 3:16,17.

The apostle Paul stated: "In fact, it says, the message is very close at hand; it is on your lips and in your heart. And that message is the very message about faith that we preach: If you openly declare that Jesus is Lord and believe in your heart that God raised him from the dead, you will be saved. For it is by believing in your heart that you are made right with God, and it is by openly declaring your faith that you are saved" (Romans 10:8-10 NLT).

Prayer and Fasting:

Jesus has given the church weapons that are mighty through God. Prayer and fasting are two powerful weapons. We can use them to cast out demons. Start praying and fasting for area of weakness. Practice casting down every negative thought, imagination, emotion, and dream. "And he said unto them, this kind can come forth by nothing, but by prayer and fasting" (Mark 9:29).

• Fasting is basically the denying of food (or something else) for a period of time. Jesus said, "If anyone wants to follow after me, let him deny himself, take up his cross daily, and follow me" (Luke 9:23 CSB)

• Prayer is your conversation with God through Jesus. Jesus told them a parable on the need for praying always and not to give up (Luke 18:1 CSB).

Fellowship with other Believers:
"And let us not neglect our meeting together, as some people do, but encourage one another, especially now that the day of His return is drawing near" (Hebrews 10:25 NLT).
The Lord said: "When two or three are gathered together in my name, I'm in the mist of them" (Matthew 18:20). Coming together with other believers will be a blessing to you. This is the kind of atmosphere that is conducive for healing. You should be able to share any concerns, and the church should encourage you through the love of Christ.

In my conclusion, this too will pass. Remember, we're living in a lifelong battle of good and evil. If you use God's Word as your strategy for spiritual warfare, you have won!
"No weapon formed against you shall prosper..." (Isaiah 54:17).
"... the joy of the Lord is your strength" (Nehemiah 8:10b).
"Your word is a lamp to guide my feet and a light for my path" (Psalm 119:105 NLT).

For if we are faithful to the end, trusting God just as we did when we first became Christians, we will share in all that belongs to Christ" (Hebrews 3:14 (TLB).

We are more than conquerors through Jesus Christ! I welcome your emails at: Pastorposton@yahoo.com

*Poetry of LOVE*

*Love is much more than a four-letter word. It's more than feelings of admiration. It's the fragrance of the soul. The hope to behold that makes one whole.*
*Come my Love; taste and see that I am great in thee. Be what I have destined you to see. Clothed with My Son, dressed in righteousness.*
*Oh, my Love, you are so beautiful to see. Like light so bright possessing life. Overcoming the night. My soul delights in the awesomeness of His light.*
*The man in me looked at the inner me.*
*Confessed the Christ in me, has gotten me the victory!*
*When the enemy desired to bury me, Love carried me; with a strength that will forever be. That's the eternal God in me.*

*By: Apostle W.L. Poston*

# Senior Chaplain Pamela R. Poston

Pastor and Evangelist Pamela Poston has professionally served her Illinois, Nevada and California communities in sales, healthcare and social services. She succeeded as an Entrepreneur, Executive Assistant, Career Coach, Case Manager, Life Skills Facilitator, and a Workforce Investment Act Program Manager.

She authored two books: Answers to Relational Healing 101 and co-authored Faith Is.

In 2006, Pamela was licensed and ordained as an Evangelist. In 2010, Evangelist Poston was ordained as a Chaplain, then later to Senior Chaplain with Messages of Faith Ministry in Las Vegas, NV. In 2011, she was ordained a Pastor through LFC-Apostolic Ecumenical Network of Kingdom Churches in Chicago, IL.

Pastor Poston is happily married and serves in ministry with her husband, Apostle Walter L. Poston of Highways & Hedges Outreach Ministries (www.Highway4JC.com). Both are Chicago, IL natives. They minister in County, Federal and State prisons and jails, to both youth and adults.

†Chapter Six

# Love Is Marriage On An Assignment

*By SR Chaplain Pamela R. Poston*

God said:

"If you are willing and obedient, you shall eat the good of the land:" (Isaiah 1:19)

As an adolescent, my family attended church regularly. As far back as I can remember, I fantasized of being in love and becoming a wife to one of the boys in church. As I grew older and met other boys, I would imagine their last names as my new last name. And to top it off, I dreamed of having a fairy-tale wedding. Then thought, if I were to have children; I would like to have twin girls.

During my internet research, I found I was not alone. Men and women alike were among this list. Some fantasized more about the engagement of popping the question; some fantasized of showing off an engagement ring to family and friends; some fantasized about a big wedding and a fun reception; while others fantasized about becoming Mrs. So-and-so. But on the other hand, others feared they would never experience this type of happiness.

Fortunately, through the grace of God, I was able to find love and have a fairytale wedding at the age of 26 with Mr. Jimmie Taylor. However, our marriage was very unstable due to our sins. We married one another three times over, trying to get it right. It was finally restored as we allowed God's restoration through obedience. However, I became a widow at the young age of 39. My detailed testimony is penned in my first book; Answers to Relational Healing 101 - Including Testimony and Teachings: How Pain Can Become Your Purpose. In this book, I share how God's faithfulness brought me through crime, emptiness, fear, homosexuality, and rebelliousness. It also includes, 78 hot topic relational healing questions and answers.

While I was still married to Jimmie, we attended church with my family in Chicago, IL. The speaker that evening was a Prophetess visiting from Milwaukee, WI. She saw me after service in the hallway and said, "God has another husband for you who will really love you very much." I explained to her after Jimmie, I never desire to marry again.

The year after Jimmie passed away, I visited my mentors' church, where a Pastor/Prophetess prophesied to me saying; "The Lord will be a source of a thousand husbands to you, before another husband comes to claim that right."

Then, years later, another Prophetess/Pastor was visiting at a different local church and she saw me in the church hallway and said, "God has a husband for you and he's a Pastor." Again, I explained to her that I was happily single as a widow and never desired to marry again. Then I shared; "I especially don't want to marry a Pastor!" Lastly, several years later at a prison ministry instructors' training, another Prophetess saw me in the hallway and said: "God has a husband for you and he's right around the corner." I again explained, "I never desired to marry again, no thank you." But GOD!

Because of my faults and failures, I vowed never to marry again. I proudly wore my wedding ring after the death of Jimmie to block any chances of male attractions. I totally embraced my celibacy of singleness. My new pursuit of fulfillment was: "I am single, saved and satisfied!" My favorite scripture became: Isaiah 54:5, "For thy Maker is thine husband; the LORD of hosts is His name..." I was now happily married to Jesus!

God was faithful to me; I desired to serve Him anyway possible. He blessed me with the gift of "Evangelism" through Jesus. I had a love and passion to share the Gospel of Christ with individuals everywhere; particularly to hurting women.

Ladies, you are so Loved by God, who will never let you down. Become intimate with Him; He's waiting on you. Intimacy is: into-me-you-see! Love loves Him who created LOVE:
"We love Him, because He first loved us." 1 John 4:19

"But God showed His great Love for us by sending Christ to die for us while we were still sinners." Romans 5:8 (TLB)

"For this is how God loved the world: He gave His one and only Son, so that everyone who believes in him will not perish but have eternal life. John 3:16 (NLT)

He allowed me to meet a wonderful couple; Apostle Thomas and Elder Esther Johnson. They along with other ministers, mentored me for years in prison ministry. As a team, we ministered in Federal, State, and County jails and prisons throughout the Chicago land areas. Shortly afterward, God told my pastor, Dr. Apostle Shaunette Houghton, to ordain me into the office of an Evangelist. After years of serving in jails and prisons; the Lord had another assignment for me.

It was now five years since Jimmie passed away. I still had not accepted any offered dates or gifts from a list of acquaintances, businessmen, and ministers. When I became a widow, my friend shared; "Girl you will be okay being single, guys will buy you meals and gifts." I vowed not to use men and especially my brothers in Christ for a meal, or to pay my bills. I did enough of this in my sins and knew that wasn't the will of God for me. I thought I was careful not to attract men or even women to myself. I was very careful not to talk with men on the phone after sundown.

For years, I fasted and prayed for God to sanctify me unto Himself (see John 17:19). The Lord was teaching me marriage lessons as I

70

devoted myself to Jesus. Without complete faithfulness, I would be cheating on Him.

My Pastor taught us marriage is ministry and we should ask our future husband; "What is your godly vision for us?" I was taught: marriage should reflect Christ and the Church; marriage should make us holy and not just happy; also, marriage is a covenant and not just a contract.

One day, I was evangelizing cell by cell at a maximum men's prison. As I walked down the prison unit tier, God told Sr. Pastor Walter L. Poston to look down the tier and there I was; walking and talking with another volunteer. I only knew him as a Senior Pastor of a local church and a prison ministry volunteer. But God had His timing in place. This reminds me of Ruth as she worked in the fields of her future husband Boaz in the book of Ruth chapters 2 and 3. Ruth served her mother-in-law Naomi with a pure heart as God was working behind the scenes in Boaz heart. Remember this saying: "Take care of God's business and He will take care of yours!"

The following year, Pastor Poston shared this with me: "I was so frightened to approach you, because at that very moment I felt love leap into my spirit!" He then left the building in fear. He felt fear because he was going through a divorce. He knew he needed time to receive the Lord's direction, forgiveness, restoration and strength before moving forward. After much prayer and counseling, God's healing and restoration took place in his heart and soul.

As we became acquainted as friends, the Lord began to press him into my heart. After some time, he shared that he was falling in love with me. I was shocked! How could this be, someone has fallen in love with me? I vowed never to marry again and to be married to Jesus until my death.

However, we met one afternoon for lunch to talk and spend time with one another. But I was still safeguarding my heart. I called my parents to share that I went to lunch with a gentleman. My mom asked with who, "JESUS"! I asked them to take a guess? Mom giggled and asked; "Is he, Pastor Poston!"?

Shortly thereafter, my parents found out the Poston family and our family lived in the same high-rise building in Chicago. They invited him over for lunch to talk more about this and share family memories. His family resided on the 16th floor and my family lived on the 10th floor. We even attended the same elementary schools. He later shared with them; "I would like to date your daughter with the intention to marry." He later met with my Pastor and shared the same.

As the Lord continued to work on me over time; He opened my heart even more. As time passed, it was a beautiful sunny crisp afternoon in Chicago. After church, Pastor Poston asked to take me to dinner. With the Lord's approval, I accepted his offer of a real date. He drove us to Navy Pier where we dined at an exclusive seafood restaurant. During dinner, we had a wonderful conversation. We enjoyed beautiful scenes of boats sailing on Lake Michigan and individuals enjoying the afternoon on the lakefront shores.

However, I noticed he seemed a bit preoccupied. Shortly after we finished our meal, he took my hand and proceeded to bend one knee toward the floor. He then pulled out a beautiful engagement ring and asked me to marry him. I was in shock! Now, by this time, the staff and guests in the restaurant noticed us. After I said, "YES" they cheered!

Now my heart was beginning to grow deeper in love, but fear of failure kept returning. I changed my mind on several occasions about being married. I made almost every excuse why I shouldn't marry again. I would hear the Lord telling me to stop refusing his marriage proposal. I did not want to give my heart away to anyone again.

God even reminded me of the four prophecies; "You will marry a man who will truly love you"; "For years, I (Jehovah-Jireh) have been your husband and now another has come to claim this right"; "You will marry a Pastor"; and "Your husband is right around the corner!" As a result, each prophecy was correct. To my surprise, he literally was in the next conference room attending the same prison ministry training.

After all these reminders from the Lord, I was still reluctant. Then the Lord asked me; "What is the ring tone on your phone?" I answered, "YES" by Shekinah Glory Ministry (God set me up with this one). Then, He said; "You will miss your blessings if you do not obey Me." I was reminded of 1 Samuel 15:22 "... obedience is better than sacrifice..." and Ruth 3:10b (TLB) "... But you have put aside your personal desires."

I had to be volun-told by God to say; "YES" to marriage again. The Lord was requiring more from me. He knew my testimony needed to be shared back in Las Vegas where the devil tried to kill, steal and destroy me. He wanted me to share how He delivered me from a prison sentence of almost 30 years for, Attempted Murder and Battery with a Deadly Weapon, especially in the County Jail where I was locked up and at the prisons where I would have served all those years. He needed me to go back into the jails and prisons to give hope to the hopeless. My presence in Las Vegas is right in the face of the devil. This reminds the enemy; "My GOD purposes will prevail!"

I later shared with my mom that I told Pastor Poston that I loved him but wasn't in love with him. I further told her, "I will marry him as an assignment to God." She wasn't happy with this news. She discerned he would be an awesome husband to me. My parents loved his genuine spirit, his gentleman demeanor and how he walks in the power of the Holy Spirit.

After a short period of dating, we sought marriage counseling. We later started sessions with three marriage counselors; of which, two are Pastors. Then, mid-spring of that year we were married in holy matrimony!

After a year of marriage, we visited Las Vegas, NV. While there, God told my husband that we were to relocate to Nevada (which is Egypt to me). Fear griped me; I was not happy with this news. After fasting, praying and consecrating for ten weeks, God confirmed this was His divine plan for us. He enlarged our territories.

We obeyed the Lord and resigned from two good jobs in 2009; during the peak of the recession. We drove through seven States to relocate to Nevada. After arriving, we found ourselves homeless and totally depending on God for His directions. This was a total "Faith Walk". My detailed testimony of this is released in the Faith Is: Inspiring Stories from Las Vegas Chaplains book.

To God be the glory; mid-spring of 2018, we celebrated 10 awesome years of marriage! I am still in awe of what I have witnessed God do through our marriage. I never knew this kind of LOVE in marriage could feel so beautiful until I said; "YES" to

God and my husband. I witnessed my parents and mentors'
awesome marriages for years but living it first hand, is bliss!

Since saying "YES", we have ministered as a couple to thousands
of souls in almost a dozen Illinois and Nevada jails and prisons. We
have evangelized on the famous Las Vegas Blvd Strip to hundreds
of souls from around the world. God has truly, enlarged our
territory and blessed us indeed; as He did for Jabez (see 1
Chronicles 4:10).

God revealed to me; "If we do things His way, we will reap His
results". The Lord also shared; "Pleasing Him is; how much of HIS
WORD we can live, not how much we can quote."

Oh, how grateful I am to have said; "'YES' to Marriage on an
Assignment!" My husband Loves the Lord and His people. He is
my best friend; he respects me; he prays for me; he's an awesome
provider; I truly Love him and like him too! I Love watching God
through him…WHEN WE LET GO AND LET GOD; WE WILL
REAP HIS REWARDS! (Isaiah 1:19)


LOVE IS

**L**ord
**O**ver
**V**ictorious
**E**xtreme

Infallible

Savior


My Lord who is victorious over the enemy's schemes (1),
demonstrated His Love to me to the extreme.

He's an infallible (2) man, who died a sinner's death on the cross
(3);
so, mankind would have the right to the tree of life (4) and not be
lost (5).

He's a Savior (6) who came to earth to demonstrate what is Love,
then the Holy Spirit descended upon Him to confirm it, like a dove.

(7) So, "Love Is" GOD (8), who sacrificed His dear Son (9);
then Jesus proved to the enemy it is finished (10) and my soul has
been won!


1. 1John 3:8
2. 1Peter 3:18
3. Romans 5:8
4. Revelation 22:14
5. 2Peter 3:9
6. Luke 2:11
7. Luke 3:22
8. 1John 4:8
9. John 3:16
10. John 19:30

# Senior Chaplain Tyrone Chew

Tyrone L. Chew, an Ordained Chaplain through Messages of Faith Ministry in May, 2016, was Ordained as a Sr. Chaplain in November, 2017. Ty retired as a Fire Captain in November 2004, proudly serving for 29½ yrs. with City of Campbell and Santa Clara County Fire Departments in California.

Ty is currently assigned to the Chaplaincy Corps with Las Vegas Fire and Rescue. Other Community Ministries include Adopt-a-Cop, Human Trafficking and Domestic Violence.

Chaplain Ty also keeps busy with Valley Vegas Church, serving on the Prayer Team; as one of the Men's Group Leaders; helping with Food Bank distribution and Las Vegas Rescue Mission; and brings occasional Encouraging Messages to Heritage Springs Assisted Living Center and Hope Chapel. He was a participating author of 'Jesus Is' and is excited to partner with 'Love Is'. Ty and his wife Sharon, who is also a Chaplain, have lived in Spring Valley since 2005.

†Chapter Seven

# Love Is The Lesson

*By SR Chaplain Tyrone Chew*


It was going to be the 'motorcycle ride to remember' in August, 2003. My buddy and I left San Jose, California, heading to Milwaukee, Wisconsin for the 100th Anniversary Celebration of Harley-Davidson. Our Colorado leg of the trip should have been a relatively easy 4 hour afternoon ride from Steamboat Springs to Ft. Collins, but because of road construction, we were detoured around the backside of the mountain. 8 hours later, we found ourselves cold, wet and tired coming up a long, uphill grade, with a chance to pass a slow moving truck hauling a horse trailer. Riding my buddy's '5', I mirrored his movement to pass and after he successfully 'dove in the hole', I found I had no room to follow. In that instant, all I saw was headlights bearing down on me! I braced myself for impact, closed my eyes and said, "oh, my God! What the ****!" And then...LOVE happened!

What is Love? For some Love is about the little things; for others it's the big things; and for a fortunate few Love is everything. For me, Love is all encompassing, and is realized through the subtle and oftentimes not so subtle, Lessons learned along the journey called Life.

On that dark, cold and wet evening, on that lonely stretch of road, with headlights bearing down on me, I realized that I was not in control! I knew in an instant that God loved me! There is no other explanation. I was definitely NOT in control of that motorcycle in that moment. When I opened my eyes I was in the right lane, coming into the curve at the top of the grade and coming down into the valley. Ft. Collins was in the far distance. I felt such great peace and calmness, seeing the clear night sky, with a multitude of stars above. Even though I have 'loud' exhaust pipes, in the 'stillness' of the moment, I heard very distinctly, "I'm not finished with you, yet!" No doubt! My life was changed forever, and it has!

Allow me to begin by stating that Life is certainly an interesting experience and NONE of us, repeat, NONE of us is getting out alive! I say this because it is a fact; that is what happens for each and every one of us – Life! Experiences – a series of events, occurrences and seasons that ingrain into each and every one of us results that mold our character over time – sometimes on a daily basis! It is an individual and dynamic process! A process as unique as our own individual fingerprints that no other person possesses!

The Bible is filled with literal and figurative Truths. Some Truths are easy to accept, but there are more than a few that are difficult to comprehend and receive. Having Faith is essential in discerning what God's Message is for us. Having Faith, I am confident about what the 40 Authors, over a period of 1,500 years, have written in the 66 Books that make up the Old and New Testaments as being accurate and essential to live Life to its fullest and completeness in Christ Jesus. My Faith and Belief in the contents and context of the Bible have had a direct and indirect influence in my past, present and future, and only God knows how long that will be! There are two essential Scripture verses that summarize Love's Lesson:

"In the beginning God created the heavens and the earth." (Genesis 1:1 NIV)

"In the beginning was the Word, and the Word was with God, and the Word was God. (John 1:1 NIV)

These two verses reveal and establish God's sovereignty and explicit Love for His work. God created ALL things for His pleasure. He provided us with the five senses that allow us to experience His Love for us – our sight, hearing, touch, smell and taste. Additionally, He allowed for us to experience free will. How we act and react to what Life presents is predicated on the choices we make. We can make good choices or we can make wrong choices. We can say yes or we can say no. We can accept or we can reject. We can live to enjoy or we can live to regret.

I am of Chinese descent and have studied the wonderful and complex culture of my ancestry. One fascinating aspect of Chinese philosophy is the principle of Yin and Yang. Represented by the symbol of a circle divided by two symmetrical 'tear drops' – one black, with a small white 'dot', and the other one white, with a small black 'dot'. The two halves represent the polar opposites of Life. Opposites that are distinct – one cannot exist without the existence of the other. Some examples: hot/cold, in/out, up/down, light/dark, bitter/sweet, fast/slow, forward/backward, happy/sad, smiles/tears, good/evil. It represents the virtual dichotomy of Life and the importance of maintaining 'Balance' and making good choices. By making good choices, Life is more peaceful and harmonious. A thin line separates the two opposites and represents how difficult it is to achieve balance, because we often live in 'extremes'! The choices we make can have benefits or they can have repercussions. It is this constant process that determines how we live every day.

In addition to the five basic senses, two others need to be briefly addressed. The first is Extra Sensory Perception. There are a few individuals who are given a gift of ESP and can express themselves beyond the parameters of the five senses – visions of the past or future (visitation, premonition and precognition). Secondly, there is Common sense – a trait that is seriously lacking in some. These unfortunate individuals are untrained and undisciplined in many aspects or their lives – and that's all I have and want to say about that!

I have found through the writings of the Bible, God's influence upon the lives of many Biblical characters. The underlying theme and emphasis of God's influence is that He is in total control. On many occasions, God could have said 'enough is enough, I've made a mistake!' But God is who He is and DOES NOT err! His unending and unlimited Grace and Mercy has shown how much Love He has for His creation. There are many examples within the Bible that are relatable to my own life and, hopefully, will direct and guide me into the future. His Forgiveness and Mercy strengthens my Faith.

With that having been said, allow me to expand on my treatise – Love Is the Lesson. One cannot read or study the Bible without realizing God had, and continues to have, a plan and a purpose for His ultimate creation – Man. From the very first to each and every one of us today, God has infused a purpose – to fulfill His plan. His plan is so utterly simple, yet it is so overlooked – Love Him and share His Love with others. This is exemplified and taught by His one and only Son, Jesus Christ, our Lord and Savior and the Holy Spirit dwelling within us.

In the beginning, God created man (and woman) in His image, to have dominion over His previous works – the earth and all the creatures that were in the skies overhead, in the waters below and those upon the land. God provided all that was necessary to take care of and benefit His creation. There was balance and Life was good! Unfortunately, the Fallen Angel, Satan, was able to tempt man and woman and cause him to disobey and turn away from God. The enemy continues even to this day to do everything within his power to seek, kill and destroy and separate us from God's Love. When exercising free will, man makes his own choices and causes imbalance. Nevertheless, God's enduring Mercy has salvaged many a life and continues to promote Hope for the future! The key is acknowledging the sin and making a declaration of confession and repentance.

"Give thanks to the Lord, for he is good. His love endures forever." Psalm 136:1 NIV

Man, without God, has stumbled repeatedly, yet learning the 'Lesson' of repentance, obedience and the Grace of God has shown what true Love is and can be. Love is multi-faceted. Love is complex. Love is the answer. If everyone could understand what Love does and can do, Life would be something to look forward to. "Love is patient, love is kind. It does not envy, it does not boast, it is not proud. It is not rude, it is not self-seeking, it is not easily angered, it keeps no record of wrongs. Love does not delight in evil but rejoices with the truth. It always protects, always trusts, always hopes, always perseveres. Love never fails."
(1 Corinthians 13:4-8a NIV)
"And now these three remain: faith, hope and love. But the greatest of these is love." (1 Corinthians 13:13 NIV)

I have an interesting hobby. I am fascinated with taking words and creating acrostics with them. It is challenging, yet satisfying. For example, CHAPLAIN:
Compassionately

Helping

And

Praying

Loving

Anyone

In

Need


In the past 2½ years, I have become a Senior Chaplain and a published Author, having participated in the second Messages of Faith Ministry book 'Jesus Is'. For this Chapter of 'Love Is", I have created the following acrostic:  LOVE

Leaving

Others

Visibly

Enlightened


I find that the process of writing this chapter has helped me grow deeper in my relationship with God and Jesus Christ and allows me to live a purposeful life.  I am fully immersed in what God has willed for me and has given me direction.  As I approach 74 years of age, my passion is not deterred.  I come to realize the gift I was given years ago has been a useful 'tool' and message to share. From the age of 12, I have been able to perform a specific type of push-up that very few can do – full extension, fingertip push-ups.  I have challenged many and have been challenged, but have never been overcome – that's over 62 years!  God Is Good!  My 'mantra':

"I can do everything through him who gives me strength."
Philippians 4:13 NIV

My past is behind me and there is nothing I can do to change that, but my future is secure in Christ Jesus. Since becoming a Chaplain and using my gift, I find that it is easier to present God and Jesus Christ to others – and isn't that the point? Everyone should know that God is real and if He can use me as proof of His existence, then I'm all in! If nothing else, it's a great ice-breaker!

I am proud to say I have served in the best capacity I could, 29½ years in the Fire Service (City of Campbell and Santa Clara County Fire Departments). I have 6 adult children from 2 previous marriages and have seen them grow to have wonderful and productive lives and marriages. I am endowed with 4 beautiful granddaughters that bring me great joy. I am married to my best friend and forever Bride, Sharon, whose 2 sons and 4 grandchildren add to my Family Treasure. I still ride my Harley, the Black Beauty 'Baby'. God is EVER so Good!

I can't say that I don't still face adversity, disappointment and pain. Far from it, I experience Life's challenges every day. I fight the adversity of temptation constantly. Living in Las Vegas presents constant temptation, but it is what it is – considered one of the major 'Entertainment Capitals of the World'. The sights, sounds and activities are ever present. I have confidence that one day 'Sin City' will be known as 'Son City'. We are working on it – one soul at a time!  I occasionally face disappointment - personal angst that what I felt ought to be isn't.  Feeling disappointed, instead of angry, has altered my perception of circumstances and has allowed me to deal with the situation in a different manner, with a different attitude.  I feel physical, mental and emotional pain more often than I'd like – the loss of loved ones, taken too soon.  Fact - Death is inevitable, I get it, and I accept that Life is in God's hands and perfect timing.  Still the pain is hard to bear.  Whenever I 'hit that wall', I am reminded to trust in the Lord –

"I have told you these things, so that in me you may have peace.  In this world you will have trouble.  But take heart!  I have overcome the world."  John 16:33 NIV)


No doubt, Life is hard!  However, what we can do is give God our very best!  If we continue to Praise and Worship Him in all things, He acknowledges us.  If we continue to Pray to Him, in silence or aloud, He hears us and understands our heart and answers every prayer with Yes, No or Not yet!  If we continue to study His Word, we gain knowledge, understanding and wisdom – Biblical maturity.  If you maintain this regimen and demonstrate these principles, peace will abide in you.

"Love the Lord your God with all your heart and with all your soul and with all your mind and with all your strength.  The second is this:  Love your neighbor as yourself.  There is no commandment greater than these."  Mark 12:29-30 NIV

All this to illustrate and say that God is Good, All the Time and All the Time, God is Good! His Love is full and complete. Allow Him to complete the work He started in you. Let go and let God!!! Know and understand that the God of all creation is real and present within us with each and every breath we take. Do not squander the gift He has given you, but willingly and openly share with others. God is gracious and kind and His Love for you is unfathomable. You may think you are unworthy and your shame and guilt unforgiveable, but you are wrong. Nothing you have done is held against you; your sins have been forgiven. Jesus Christ paid the debt for your sins by dying on the cross. He defeated death by rising from the tomb on the third day, promising an eternal life with God in Heaven to those who believe. Believe it and receive it!

In conclusion, my desire is that you realize how important you are to God. Know that you are here and who you are because God intended you to be here and be who you are. You are unique and special in His eyes. Know that you mean something to God and have great worth and purpose. You may not know it now, just put your trust in Him. He so Loves You.

"Do not conform any longer to the pattern of this world, but be transformed by the renewing of your mind. Then you will be able to test and approve what God's will is – his good, pleasing and perfect will. "Romans 12:2 NIV
Love Is the Lesson!!!

# Senior Chaplain Shirley Davis

SR Chaplain Shirley established the Nevada non-profit prayer ministry, "Prayer 4 U 2, Ministries" in 2017. A native Nevadan, SR Chaplain/Minister Shirley Davis-Hollins has built her life and career around principles that God has instilled in her such as a dedication to ministry. Married to Terry Hollins, she has three sons, 15 grand- children, and one great grand-child. With this foundation, she has been made strong in Christ and has accumulated many accolades.

Sr Chaplain/Minister Davis-Hollins is a member of Victory Missionary Baptist Church, pastored by Dr. Robert Fowler Sr, for over 30 years, and is currently involved in the seniors, and guest ministry, as well as the children's church. She is an MOFM ordained SR Chaplain and Academy Graduate. She is a member of the Adopt -a-Cop NV ministry and a rescue ministry member who takes in homeless women and children through recovery centers.

Her religious education includes theology training from Dr. Fowler at Victory, and has a formal education from the College of Southern Nevada.

Sr Chaplain/Minister Shirley Davis retired as Assistant Vice President from Nevada State Bank, with 25 years of dedication, and with 2 years of international banking in Japan. After retiring she felt a calling to assist special needs children and had worked for eight years as a bus aide for CCSD. With all this, she plans to keep strong in faith and go and teach what God assigns to her.

†Chapter Eight

# †Love Is The Source of My Strength

*By SR Chaplain Shirley Davis*

Love is the source of my strength! Without the strength of God to help me through this journey of life, I would be nothing! I found out without God, . I wouldn't have the joy of the Lord to give me the strength to move forward. God's joy is like none other. The world defines joy as someone or something that places a smile on your face for a short time. But the joy of the Lord has an everlasting source that bubbles up even when things look against you. The strength of the Lord arises and places a smile upon your face and you know without a doubt God got it all in His hand. I read it in his word John 16:22, the world didn't give it and the world cannot take it away,

The Joy that I have has given me the strength to go on when I'm tired of the fight that we are in each and every day. I found out that my joy in the Lord is my weapon! When I praise Him when things go right or when they go wrong. I know God is in the plan. It does not matter what the situation looks like, praise God! Praise Him because He is God and He along is worthy to be praised! Satan can't stand it when you praise God regardless of the outcome.

I've learned to trust Him with my every direction. For in Psalms 37:23, it reads. "The steps of a man are established by the Lord, when he delights in his way." I believe the Bible, if you do what the Lord says, he will make certain each step you take is sure. Don't you want to be sure in your steps? I do, if I'm living for the Lord. I tried it my way too many times. Each time I tried it, it just got worse. It finally got so bad that I said, God forgive me, can we start over?

He knows my past, my todays and my tomorrow's. God had to show me how well he knew me. He showed me working as a grocery store cashier (in a vision). When He came into the store walking around, I spotted him. He got in my line and he had several people go before him and I wondered why he was doing that, and when he finally got up to me, he said, that he was the Lord. I asked him, what took you so long to come up to me. He said when I was next, you still were not ready to receive me, and so I let others ahead of me. And now that I've got your attention, you were concerned about what people would say about you since they knew of your past. He said, if they remind you about your past, tell them to come and talk with him. He said, all those folks I let through before me, I know what they were carrying and all those after me; I know what they carry as well. He said, now you belong to me, and tell them about me and if they want to know anything about you come to me. That pleased me. I know He loves me and has me in His care. That's why I trust Him. He loves me despite of what others might say. I know without a doubt He loves me.

In 1 John 4:19 It says, "We love him, because he first loved us." When I read that tears began to roll down my face because I knew nobody could ever love me as the Lord does.

I have been in love in the world way too many times, thinking that I got it right each time. The love of God I didn't know, and he said that he would show me how to love the godly way starting with Him. In Matthews 22:37-39, "And said unto him, you shall love the Lord your God with all your heart, and with your soul, and with all your mind. This is the greatest commandment. A second is equally important: Love your neighbor as yourself". The entire law and all the demands of the prophets are based on these two commandments.

I had to put myself in check. I didn't love like that! Why? I made a promise to myself and the devil put a big check mark right there. He thought he had me, because I was on my way to do what I wanted to do. Why? Because it's my thing, and I do what I want to do. Remember that song, it was hot in the 70's when women were gaining back their rights as women. But God, He had another plan for me. He wanted to make sure I knew what love really is. The bible tells us all about love. I found out love starts with God. I Corinthians 13:1-8. Loves begins and never ends. I finally got it! You cannot love correctly until you truly love God first.

As time went on my desire to work in the community grew. I prayed and ask God to show me where to get started in the community. The Lord pointed me to a very good friend of mine who told me about a ministry that has several ministries for the community, The Messages of Faith Ministries. I joined and love it. I have been a member since 2016 and have fallen in love with the officers and members of this ministry. And now I am in love with the ministries of Help.

While working with my church and Messages of Faith Ministries. God spoke to my heart to open a new monthly ministry, Me an Entrepreneur! I had a strong desire to help Gods people. I started a business of faith, a non-profit ministry to help the community to be empowered to pray for themselves, their families, the community and the world. Last year the ministry focused on Prayer. 13 individuals attended sessions on prayer and they all received a prayer shawl for completing the "Prayer Journey" sessions. At the end of the session, we had a wonderful dinner celebration. Can't wait to see what God is going to do in 2019.

Serving God changed my life completely. As a native of Las Vegas, I've seen Las Vegas change its course from being a place to vacation with your kids to leaving the kids at home for their safety. Las Vegas is a place for adult's entertainment. Entertainment with casinos for gambling to shows only adults should see. I had my first real job when I turned 21 in the casinos. I worked there for 2 years and I moved on knowing the casino life wasn't for me. As a child of a minister, I knew the casinos we here for adult entertainment and a place where your choice to take a change with either winning a little money to losing your life savings. Working in a bank for over 28 years, I tell new residents to be careful living here in Vegas. This place can make your love stronger or it can break up a happy home with the 24-hour activities of gambling, drugs, drinking or partying all night long.

In our house, as a child, my parents were involved in our everyday life. Our mother didn't work so she was home every day when our father worked hard to raise 7 children. We had everything we needed. We had love from both parents who guided us with Godly principles. I remembered our father sending our mother on a vacation every summer. She went home to visit her mother in her home town. As a child, we were glad to see mom leave because we now could spend more time with our friends, cousins and the neighborhood kids. Our father would take us swimming and camping with our friends almost every week. But our life changed one month after my 16th birthday. Our father was murdered on the 4th of July and that changed our life completely. Our mother was left to raise 5 children. Ages ranged 17 years to 18 months old baby. Not only did our life change but it affected the entire community.

I felt the love leave our family. We were all lost, our mother without a husband and 7 children without a father. Life, as we knew, took a toll on all of us. Just turning 16 with my first boyfriend I felt like love had changed my life. I began to look for love in all the wrong places. I didn't turn to God I turned to the world, looking for someone to fill that love gap that was missing from my heart. I was very close to our father. I was the one who would run to retrieve his lunch box to see what was left inside just for me. Every day our father knew who would greet him when he got home, I did. Now I wasn't seeing his face coming home from a long day of work to his loving family. The love of our father was missing from his entire family.

Our mother was trying to deal with raising children alone and we were now facing adulthood from what we knew. As I grew up I got married at the age of 17. One year after our father's death. Now, I depended on the world to give me the love that I was missing. I got pregnant by my first boyfriend. I didn't know my husband nor was I was ready for marriage. We decided to go in different directions, and I didn't know how to handle it since I was pregnant. I just ran away from it all.

I divorced him and decided to move on with my life with my loving 10.2 pound baby boy. The only plan that I had was that I was going to keep loving, and if another man stops loving me I would leave him too. I was heading in the direction that pleased satan, not God. I felt alone. But had to move on and raise my son the best way that I could. I married again 6 years later, and I had another handsome son. That husband was into drugs; which he had a drug problem before marrying me. He was from New York and in the military. After the drugs became a part of our life I tried to deal with it. We attended counseling. It didn't work so I divorced him.

Life went on, but now I had two sons. I began going to church and started serving God, not in or having a relationship with God but serving Him.

I got married again. This time I thought I picked the right man. This man decided I wasn't the right one for him while we were in Okinawa Japan. Again, I said to God, I am tired, tired of making the wrong decisions. That's when God spoke to me. He said I've been here waiting for you. I cried and asked God to forgive me. Right then I decided to turn completely over to God. He told me, I love you. And the next time that I married out of His Will the marriage would be very abusive. I said ok Lord. One thing I knew that I didn't want was another abusive relationship. That changed me completely.

I was determined to regain my strength. I was determined to seek God with my whole heart! I learned to speak up for myself with the help of God to give me the strength to do so. Life in God is sweet! At the age of 35 I began to know who I was in Christ Jesus. It took over 25 years for me to have the right godly man in my life. I was 54, enjoying the life as a single woman. I didn't know God has a sense of humor! I met my husband on a plane. He was sitting right next to me. He lived in Michigan and I lived in Las Vegas. I took my great nephew and great-niece to visit their grandma and my sister in Ohio. The nearest airport to Las Vegas was from Detroit. This flight was heading to Las Vegas. My husband was on that plane sitting next to me. He was going to Vegas to visit friends and looking to move to Las Vegas once his job opened up for transfer. He was the next in line for job transfer after a two-year wait. We married two years later. I moved to Michigan for 4 years. The transfer came through after a 7-year wait. Now we are both at my church home of 30 years, both serving in the house of the Lord for over 8 years now. I am a minister and my husband is a deacon at Victory Missionary Baptist Church.

Therefore, love is God. God is love. Without the love of God, I wouldn't know how to love correctly. The world's way is temporary love. It fades away like a lovely rose. It smells good for a while but slowly fades. The Love of God grows and grows into a lovely blooming rose to leave its scent wherever it goes and its destination is with the Lord.

God's love is perfect, faithful, unconditional, forgiving, all-encompassing, pure, lasting, sacrificial, strong, enduring, refreshing, redeeming, everlasting, lavish, full, inspiring, hope-filled, gracious, and so much more. It's never based on us, our abilities, or striving to ever be good enough. It's found in Him, his character, and a high capacity to give. It knows no boundaries and has no limits. There's no place too deep that His love can't reach us still.

Therefore, love is my strength to love others as He loves me. In the Bible, it speaks on love. 1 Peter 4:8 says: Above all, love each other deeply because love covers a multitude of sins. How can I say, I love you? It's through Jesus. Our Lord our God who loves us first. Then I stop and think, God had patience with me, I need to have patience with others and patience with myself. I believe, if we all take the time to look into the heart of every soul we will find Jesus waiting just like he waited for us.

At times when I feel that I can't go on and my strength grows weak, I spend time with God and he reminds me to put my thoughts and my mind on him and realize it's not my strength or love or power but His. It gives me the courage to get up and go on. His name, that name that gives me strength from day to day, and it will never lose its power.

# Senior Chaplain Gracie Spaight

Gracie Spaight is a mother of three beautiful children; she is also a grand mother of seven. She started out as a Sunday School Teacher, Singing in the Choir, and in the Mission Field. She was a Chaplain with Sunrise Hospital, and with the (formerly known as) Southern Nevada Hospital. Gracie demonstrated Love on the Aids Ward, Children's Ward, and Cancer Ward, as well as with Street and Park Ministry, while winning souls for the Kingdom of God, Marriage Conference, and Single's Conference.

Gracie was later Ordained and Licensed as an Evangelist by Nathan Whitney, in March of 2002, God has graced her to share in Men and Women ministries doing the work of an Evangelist. She has served in the North Las Vegas Woman Jail, Smiley Road Prison. Gene Nevada Prison, Down Town Jail, and doing the work of a Church Administrator, She became a Senior Chaplain with MOFM in Nevada. She is currently a volunteer at the West Care Women and Children's Rehabilitation Center in Las Vegas. Gracie also a NV State licensed Wedding Officiate, and available to perform the sacraments of Baptism, and Funeral Services, In Jesus Name.

†Chapter Nine

# Love is Powerful

*By SR Chaplain Gracie Spaight*

Abuse comes in a variety of ways, but the most common are: physical, verbal, psychological, and sexual. Many of us have experienced one or all at some point in our lives. I have experienced them all.

I share my story to encourage you with whatever you are going through. You are not alone, and nothing is impossible for God, Everything I experienced chased me into the arms of God. Writing my life story has stirred in me deep rooted feelings and questions I never thought about before. It has caused me to feel some type of way. Putting words to these feelings are difficult for me. Have you ever felt like the hound dogs from Hell were on your trail to destroy you? Have you ever felt like you were born into a family you didn't ask for or feeling as if you were reaping the sins your parents sowed?

I am the third child of eight siblings, my mother made sure we went to church on Sunday mornings. We lived on a farm in Tallulah Louisiana; my grandfather was a full-blooded Apache Indian, who provided for our family, he was the meanest man I have ever known. He never attended church that I know of or spoke about Jesus. He was the closest man to me while I was growing up. My grandmother had 14 children. Can you imagine your grandmother having children the same time as one of her daughters? We had four families living under one roof, so the children slept four to a bed. The other families in the area lived miles away, so my cousins were all I knew. The spirit of incest ran rapid in the household, with my grandfather, uncles, aunts, brothers and sisters. I was molested at the age of six years old by my uncles until I was twelve years old. Those famous words, don't tell no one, this is our little secret. I have heard people ask the question, "Why does God allow bad things to happen to children? This is a very difficult question to answer.

God is never the instigator of abuse. The scripture "James 1:13 says, Let no man say when he is tempted, I am tempted of God, For God cannot be tempted with evil, neither tempted he any man. I grew up thinking that this was the only way of living. Surrounded by darkness, no one in the house really knew who Jesus was. That ugly spirit of abuse has a way of following you. Another encounter with abuse happened with my math teacher. She would call on me to answer a problem and if I didn't know the answer, she would take a strap and whip me every time. This made the other kids in the class make fun of me. I was so embarrassed and terrified to go to school. She traumatized me. I had no one I could talk to about this. There was no one to help me. All I could do was cry.

Things were so bad in my grandparent's house because there were so many people living there. I remember my grandfather and mother getting into these horrible fights. He would make her leave the house in the rain or snow. I witnessed my mother having a nervous breakdown. She acted as if she had lost her mind. It was something no child should have to witness. One day my mother packed up her children and we left my grandparent's house. The house we moved into, at night, you could see the stars through the roof. I believe God gave us a break from the ugly darkness that surrounded us.

I watched my mother depend on God for everything. I remember hearing her crying out to God asking him to send food for her children to eat. The next morning food was coming from everywhere. People were bringing clothes, water etc. It was wonderful; we loved each other so much. We didn't know we were poor until later in life. My mother worked so hard to take care of us. Then one day she told us she was going to leave us with our grandmother to go to Las Vegas to start a new life for us. We begged her not to leave us. It seemed like the end of the world had come hearing those words. She took us back to our grandparent's house where the devil himself was waiting on us. I was so angry with my mother. "The scripture, 1Peter 5:8 says, "Be sober, be vigilant, because your adversaries the devil as a roaring lion walks about seeking whom he may devour. And "Proverbs 4:19 says, "The way of the wicked is like darkness, they do not know over what they stumble."

My mother left us and went to Las Vegas Nevada. My life turned for the worse, the spirit of abuse was still in my path. My grandfather taught us how to light his peace pipe; in return, I started smoking and stealing cigarettes. My grandmother would let us taste her beer. The worst was yet to come. I didn't know at the time that I was acting out the feeling of abandonment. I had the biggest hole in my heart. It left me numb, it didn't matter if I was getting molested or not. I decided to join in with the crowd where ever I could fit in. I thought my mother would never come back to get us, but after three years she returned for us. She had a big surprise for us. He was a six feet tall man with a perm on his head. He was city slick, and thought he was pretty boy Floyd.

There was something about him that didn't feel right. Only children can discern that spirit. I didn't like him and neither did my grandfather. I left Tallulah Louisiana at the age of thirteen. That same spirit of abuse followed me to Las Vegas. The feeling about my stepfather came true. My mother felt comfortable leaving my sister and I at the house with him. The next night he came in my room tried to molest me. I woke up to his hands fondling me. I jumped up and he ran from the room. There was no more sleep for me that night. When my mother returned home, I didn't tell her. I guessed it was the norm. There would be no chance for him and me to build a relationship.

The devil had a plan for me, but he didn't know the Lord Jesus Christ had a plan for me too. He didn't know I would be leaving his kingdom going to the kingdom of God. "Jeremiah 29:11 says, "For I know the plans I have for you declares the Lord, plans to prosper you and not to harm you, plans to give you hope and a feature." Ezekiel 36:26 says, "A new heart also will I give you, and I will put a new spirit within you; and I will take away the stony heart out of your flesh, and I will give you a heart of flesh."

I became hard hearted and numb, I was so angry. I couldn't tell my mother what happened. I could still hear my uncle's voice as a child saying, "Don't tell nobody, this is our secret. It is between us and us only." As the years passed by, I became sexually active. This time it was not with relatives, it was with whomever. When I left the South I was only smoking cigarettes, this was nothing compared to what I was introduced to in Las Vegas. I was introduced to marijuana; this devil really had a plan for me. How many of you know that drugs are not free? Well, it was free to me for a while.

Drugs started coming from everywhere. I had no problem with abusing my body with substances. I remember I would go to school so high sitting in class doing nothing, I was not able to stay in a normal class room, they moved me to special education, I still could not keep up, my brain could not contain the school work, it was so embarrassing to go to that class, I would sneak in when no one was looking. I would copy off other student's paper to get a passing grade. I met my husband in school. He took me to my prom and school games. I did receive a diploma, all though I didn't have an education, my mom was so proud of me.

The spirit of abuse was still controlling my life. We dated for three years before he touched my hand. For the first time I thought a man loved me. We really did enjoy each other's company. Our relationship was healthy, no sex was involved. The use of drugs did not stop. He became a dope dealer. The drugs where for real free now. The devil knows just how to do it. My mother had no idea that I was using drugs like I was. She grew to like my boyfriend. I had no idea the importance of having an education. The only job I could get was being a maid at a motel that paid $6.00 an hour.

As time went by, still doing drugs, partying all night, my boyfriend had other plans for us. He decided he wanted to get intimate, and we ended up one night having sex. Now we felt as if we belonged to each other. I did not know what was waiting for me. One night he came over, and I said something he didn't like. He hit me in my face. I turned and hit him back. He then grabbed me and slammed me on my back on the floor knocking the breath out of me. I cried so hard, the spirit of abuse was still haunting me. He left my house and I didn't see him for a couple of weeks. Something began to happen to my body, so I went to the doctor. When he told me I was with child, my mouth was wide open. The only thing I could think about was that night of the fight when he slammed me on my back. I didn't think about it anymore. Going into the third month, I had a miscarriage.

Losing the baby drove me into deep a depression. I began to abuse my body all over again. Although we were still dating, my heart was so empty from the loss of the baby. I felt like a walking corpse. I felt so empty. I started doing enough drugs for two people. I started going to the stores stealing whatever I got my hands on. It didn't matter what it was. I didn't care. I think if I had died, I would have lifted my eyes in hell. Yes, I was hell bound. My mouth became a mouth piece for Satan. I cursed like an 80-year-old woman from the deep parts of the South. I would fight anybody who looked like they wanted to fight. I became a gang member. I turned Las Vegas inside out.

My mother had no idea what type of person I had become. She was busy fighting her own demons. The man she married turned out to be an abuser. They were fighting every other night. All her time was geared towards him. She didn't know my boyfriend had turned out to be so abusive just like the man she married until one day I told her how he was. She began to tell me the things her husband was doing to her. My heart was broken. I could not believe my ears. It was like the two of them were brothers. My mother told me not to marry my boyfriend. I did not listen to her. I believe my mom set her heart to start praying for me. She knew I was in trouble.

I was with child once again. This time the pregnancy was carried full term. Why wasn't there anyone in my life ministering to me?

Where were the Christians? My whole life changed after having my baby. The process of me surrendering my life to Jesus was at work. The lord was calling me. I felt like I was a grown woman. My life had changed, and I was different. I had to change for the baby's sake.

I started going to church frequently, but I was not completely committed yet. I heard the preacher preaching on fornication, that I was going to hell if I would not stop. I was convicted. I told my boyfriend he could not touch me again unless he married me, and he did. My heart began to change towards God. I stopped doing the drugs, while still smoking cigarettes. Now I am living in a house with this man who I call my husband. I became his punching bag every other weekend.

My life was a living hell. I had three children living in this nightmare with me. All he ever talked about was finding ways to kill me. They watched the good and the bad, the ugly. There were times when my children enjoyed their father, but for them to be watching their mother being abused regularly broke my heart. We dreaded the weekend. Someone asked me why I didn't leave him? I thought I loved him, I wanted him to change, I thought he was going to change, he didn't want to change. After sixteen years of being in the abusive relationship, I discovered the spirit of abuse can be a deadly addiction. You become addicted to the abuse until you get delivered.

One day I decided I wanted out. My relationship with the Lord was solid; I began to understand his love for me. His love saved my life, His loved redeemed my soul. His love protected me. The scripture that comes to mind is " Psalms 34:6, This poor man cried, and the Lord heard him and saved him out of all his troubles, " Psalms 40:2 says, " He brought me up out of the pit of destruction, out of the miry clay and he set my foot upon a rock making my footsteps firm."

He delivered me from that abusive relationship; He is using me to bring Glory to his name. My goal is to reach as many women and men in this trap of being abused and introduce them to the Kingdom of God.

I begin to use his powerful word to show others how to live a peaceful life. Living in that abusive relationship was not Gods plan for me. The more I read my bible; the Holy Spirit would open my eyes to truth. I received his truth and I was set free.
God's love is powerful.

# Senior Chaplain Carol Tidd

Carol Tidd was ordained as a Chaplain in November 2016 and graduated as a Senior Chaplain in November 2017. Carol was part of the Chaplaincy Nevada response to the 1 October shootings and is also a member of the Nevada State Chaplain Task Force.

Carol attends The Crossing Church where she serves as a leader for Celebrate Recovery and as a prayer counselor for baptism events. Carol is a volunteer with the Las Vegas Metropolitan Police Department, a member of the Las Vegas Mayor's Faith Initiative Human Trafficking team, and has participated in multiple missing children searches with Nevada Child Seekers and Free International.

Carol is also involved in RECAP (Rebuilding Every Community Around Peace), which connects local law enforcement and the faith community to bring healing to the Las Vegas communities impacted by racial, gang, or other incidents.

Carol is thankful for the grace of God in her life.

# Chapter Ten

# Love Is Redemption

*By SR Chaplain Carol Tidd*

Grace was a bunny that was born in a small town in Ohio. She enjoyed playing in the grass, woods, and orchards near her home. Her home was very small and Grace preferred playing outside whenever she could. In the warm months, Grace would spend hours climbing trees and exploring the areas around her home. In the winter, she learned to ice skate and loved playing in the snow. Sometimes, her big brother Dave would let her play with him and his friends. Dave would tease her but Grace knew that he loved her and that he would protect her. Grace felt safe and comfortable in her little family. She had both sets of grandparents including aunts, uncles, and cousins that lived nearby. They enjoyed spending time at each other's houses. She loved to remember family cookouts by the nearby lake, picnics at the park, and going to cabins for long weekends in the Spring and Fall. She was the youngest of all the cousins so she was the center of attention for her parents and family.

As she got older and started to attend school, her family dynamics began to change. Her Grandma Hazel became very ill and was put in the hospital. The last time Grace saw Grandma Hazel was outside in the parking lot, waving towards her from her hospital window. The next day, she was told that Grandma Hazel had died. Grace didn't understand what happened and was confused by the sadness. Soon after this, her big brother Dave moved far away and she rarely saw him. Shortly after Dave left, her Grandpa Harry who had just lost his wife came to stay with her family. Grandpa Harry was very sad and Grace had to be quiet in the house because she wasn't supposed to disturb him. Grace was frustrated that she had to be quiet as well as behaving at school just to come home to do more of the same thing. Grace was no longer the center of attention, and didn't understand what was going on in her world. Because she was so much younger than her cousins, there were times she was pushed aside, as the rest of the family dealt with "adult" things.

Then, Grace's other Grandma, Mamie, became ill. This was different than what happened with Grandma Hazel. Grandma Mamie became very forgetful and kept calling Grace hurtful names or yelling at her for things she hadn't done. Grace sweetly remembered how Grandma Mamie used to invite her into the kitchen to help, talking to her about cooking and other activities. Eventually, Grandma Mamie had to move to another place where she could be taken care of because Grandpa Floyd could no longer take care of her needs adequately. One again, Grace didn't understand what was going on in her world.

There were older rabbits around Grace all the time, not only her family. She was still the baby, but started looking less cute as she got older. Her eyes crossed and she had to wear ugly, thick glasses. She was teased all the time by other rabbits and called mean names. Grace told her parents but they dismissed it and told her it was part of growing up. Grace often played by herself and she loved to read books. Books took her to different places, showing her families that did things together and to her eyes showed they loved each other. Grace imagined herself being in the books, living a different life. Because she read all the time, the reading classes at school were easy for her and her classmates teased her because she did too well for their liking. The teasing made Grace withdraw more and more into her books that provided a world where she felt safe and comfortable.

About the same time, a rabbit everyone called Kennedy became a leader in the small town. Everyone loved and admired Kennedy. He had bunnies about Grace's age. Sadly, a farmer shot Kennedy one day when he was out in a park. The community was devastated, and Grace saw Kennedy's bunnies looking so miserable and crying. Grace didn't understand what had happened and why everyone was so very, very sad, it was just like when her Grandma Hazel died.

Grace continued to grow up and felt more and more isolated from her family and didn't have any close friends. At the same time, her Daddy who she loved very much was spending more and more time with her alone. She liked the attention but felt that her Mommy should be doing things with her and her Daddy and not being left out. She saw other families do things together and thought that was what should be happening in her family. Sometimes when she was alone with her Daddy, he would touch Grace and it made her feel good, but he told her not to ever tell her Mommy or any other grownups because this was their secret.

Grace started having nightmares and would wake up screaming and crying. Instead of comforting her, her parents told her to be quiet and not to wake them up. Grace's teachers told Grace's Mommy that they were seeing changes in her but nothing changed at home. Grace continued to do well in school even as the situation at home continued. She learned what it took to keep the peace at home and how to make friends, especially with boys. The boys liked her, especially when she would let them touch her like her Daddy had been doing for a long time. She thought it was what a girl was supposed to do, especially when she heard about her classmates doing the same things. She felt bad sometimes for doing what she was doing but it kept her away from home and made others happy.

During these important years in Grace's life, her Grandpa Harry and Grandma Mamie died after being sick for a long time. Her Grandpa Floyd died not long after Grandma Mamie, and her aunts and uncles said he died of a broken heart. Grace didn't understand what they meant and asked how is heart could be broken when he looked OK to everyone around him.

After several years, Grace moved away, got married, and started
her own family. Grace still felt like she didn't fit in, even with the
other young moms, she felt sad most of the time. During this time,
her big brother Dave got really sick and died far away from where
Grace lived. Grace was not able to see him and say goodbye
before he died.

Grace's friends started telling her about another rabbit named Billy
and that he would sometimes come and visit and made the rabbits
feel hopeful. They said Billy knew this man named Jesus and that
He was good. Grace didn't understand how a man could give hope
because her Daddy had hurt her and some of the boys in her life,
which made her, become scared of them. She remembered that a
man killed Kennedy when she was a child, thinking all men must
be bad if they can do so many harmful things. Grace was able to
take her babies with her to go see Billy when he came to speak.
Billy was able to tell stories and help her understand more and
more about this man named Jesus. Grace was excited and wanted
to learn more. Billy said Jesus had lived a long time ago, had been
killed and had come back to life and could live in her heart. Grace
found some other rabbits that liked to learn about Jesus and started
spending time with them. Some of the rabbits made her feel
valued and she really liked them. She also felt like she could be
herself around them.

Grace continued to spend time learning about Jesus and changes in her heart and her life began to change. She is starting learning that Jesus could redeem and restore her painful past. But, she was afraid that He would somehow let her down or punish her because of things that had happened to her and the things she had done. She believed in her heart that she was damaged and that not even Jesus could fix her and restore her. She felt that Jesus would do that for others, but not for her.

Grace's bunnies were growing up and her life looked pretty good to everyone around her. But, Grace's husband Rick was getting sadder and angrier as time went on. No matter what Grace did, it didn't make things better at home. Grace loved Rick very much and it broke her heart to see him turn into a different rabbit than the one she fell in love with.

Grace's life was forever changed when more deaths happened in her family. After her brother, then it was the aunt and uncle that had lived closest to her family, her father within a few months, and her mother the following year. Grace had Jesus in her life but the deaths really impacted her. Meanwhile, her husband Rick was slipping further and further away and didn't support her as she was dealing with a great deal of pain due to all the deaths in her family. Once again, Grace felt abandoned by her family and those that were supposed to love and support her.

Grace and her family had the opportunity to move near the mountains and make big changes in their lives. Grace was excited to get away from some bad influences and make a fresh start. But the old pain and loneliness followed her to the mountains. Grace's husband Rick got more and more angry and began to withdraw from their relationship. Grace couldn't help him, no matter what she did. Grace began spending as much time as she could with him, thinking that would help the marriage, but she was miserable.

Finally, Grace got the strength to walk away from the marriage and start a new life. She got involved with other rabbits that loved Jesus and they proved that they loved her and were truly there for her. Grace started feeling better and more hopeful. Grace's new friends explained to her that her that her name came from the word 'grace', derived from the Latin 'gratia', meaning God's favor. Grace always had felt her name was a curse because she was anything but graceful as a child and wanted to hide and not draw any attention to herself. To be told over and over again that her name meant God's favor was something that Grace really wanted to believe was true, and eventually her heart and mind accepted the truth of her new life. Grace accepted the redemption that only Jesus could offer. She understood, finally, these verses from Colossians 1:13-14: "For He rescued us from the domain of darkness, and transferred us to the kingdom of his beloved son, in who we have redemption, the forgiveness of sin."

She began to help other rabbits with things like giving out food and clothes, and even sitting down and talking to them and helping them with their problems. Sometimes, Grace would speak to rabbit meetings and share her story and give them hope that in spite of all she had been through, she was now not only surviving but also thriving.

Grace learned to trust Jesus with everything in her life after so many years of feeling alone and mistreated. She was no longer the scared rabbit who wanted to run away to live in the fantasy world of her books. And, she learned that she had friends that had proven themselves to be trustworthy, and this included many men. Grace finally understood who she was in Jesus, and that she was deeply and fully loved by Jesus and that she had close friends that loved her and had proven they would be there for her.

Joel 2:25-27 from the Old Testament became real in Grace's life: 25 "I will repay you for the years the locusts have eaten—the great locust and the young locust, the other locusts and the locust swarm—my great army that I sent among you. 26 You will have plenty to eat, until you are full, and you will praise the name of the LORD your God, who has worked wonders for you; never again will my people be shamed. 27 Then you will know that I am in Israel, that I am the LORD your God, and that there is no other; *never again will my people be shamed.*"

Grace was able to walk forward without shame, with a purpose, and with hope for an amazing future.

# Senior Chaplain Lovie Ringgold

SR Chaplain Lovie lives in Las Vegas, Nevada. She was born in Memphis Tennessee and later moved to Los Angeles California.

She was employed, and retired from the United States Postal Services after thirty years.

She has been a member of the Victory Missionary church for fifteen years, and serves as a greeter.
She completed a two year studies in Evangelism and graduated in 2016.

She has been an ordained Chaplain with Messages of Faith Ministry for three years, and graduated from its Chaplaincy Nevada Academy as a SR Chaplain.

†Chapter Eleven

# Love Is Understanding

*By SR Chaplain Lovie Ringgold*

Dear Lord: As I ask the Holy Spirit to guide my thoughts to pen and then to paper, that my story will be a help to the person or the persons who read this book. Love Is Understanding.

Born in Memphis, Tennessee I was the oldest of my six brothers and sister. My father was a deacon and we had to attend church regularly. At the age of ten I accepted Christ as my Lord and Savior and was baptized. I did, however, have a vision of angels playing on a staircase leading up to heaven. I told my mother about it that morning, she had no answer for me. I didn't know what it was to have a relationship with Christ until later in life.

"Train up a child in the way he should go; and when he is old, he will not depart from it." Proverbs 22:6.

At the age of thirteen my father and mother wanted a better life for their children. My father got a job in Los Angeles, California; this was to become our new home. Everything was good until I started high school. At this young age I was being persuaded to smoke cigarettes. I tried it, but it was not for me. I didn't do drugs, but I did try alcohol. I was not promiscuous; I was a country girl trying to be a city girl. By eleventh grade I became sexually active and pregnant. I tried to hide my pregnancy from everyone until one day my dad asked me if I was expecting. I told him yes. My parents had suspected that I was pregnant by the changes in my body. I was taken to the doctor and it was confirmed. I was pregnant, but I pressed my way through high school, through home school, and I eventually graduated. As a young mother with a young baby I was unskilled and unable to get a job. My mother took me to social services. I was approved and had some form of support besides my parents.

Although I had a child out of wedlock experiencing pain and embarrassment my trust in the father of my child was regained. We got married and I became pregnant with our second child. Being a young married couple, our marriage was not good, we later divorced.

"For I know the plans I have for you, declares he Lord, plans for welfare, and not for evil, to give you a fortune and a hope."
Jeremiah 29:11

My children were getting older and I wanted to do more for them. I started job hunting, as unskilled as I was; I stated working for a temporary agency. This lasted for a while. I finally took the test for United States Postal Service and passed it and I was hired. I finally had a good job. My son left from under my leadership and he became an atheist. All praises to God, he and his sister are now born- again believers. Still looking for love in all the wrong places.

The devil knew how to set me up, so I met my second husband who worked for the postal service. We had two children, the kids and I went to church and he did not. He and I were unequally yoked. "Do not be unequally yoked together with unbelievers. For what fellowship has righteousness and lawlessness? And what communion has light with darkness." 2 Corinthians 6:14. By not knowing or adhering to the word of God I caused myself a lot of grief, pain and heartache unnecessarily. Had I really known his way I believe my life at that time could have been much better. "Trust in the Lord with thine heart and lean not unto thine own understanding. In all thy ways acknowledging him, and he will direct thy paths." Proverbs 3:5-6. I still had not learned to allow God to lead me or guide my footsteps in life, nor had I learned from previous relationships about trusting God.

I am divorced again! "Thus he will sprinkle many nations, Kings will shut their mouths on account of him; for what had not been told them they will see, and what they had not heard they will understand." Isaiah 52:15. Needing a change, my last two children and I moved to Las Vegas, Nevada. My only sister and her son moved to Nevada. Nevada is where I met my third husband which is to be my last husband.

It was my birthday and I had talked to my sister about my birthday plans. She told me she had a gift for me that she did not wrap. I told her I wasn't doing much just cooking my favorite foods, and that was about it, I told her to just drop off my gift in case she had to work. Later that evening she came by, but not by herself. My gift was a man who later became my husband. I was totally surprised by this, and I invited them both in. After exchanging introductions, we began to talk, and they wished me happy birthday. There was an immediate connection between him and me. We were being overly polite and even shy. We had dinner, and my sister left, and he stayed behind a little longer. This was the beginning of our whirlwind relationship. We spent all our time together and in one month and nineteen days we got married. I guess I could say I (we) fell in love at first sight.

I certainly had not taken the time to get to really know about him and he had not taken the time to get to know me either. For better or worse, words which are a part of the marriage vows, and just as I had said "I do" before in my previous marriages, I was once again repeating them. Did they now have a different meaning to me? However, the worst was yet to come from this instant connection. We settled into roles of being husband and wife, but our life together began to change. He finally told me he had retired from the army and had gotten hit in the back with a tank and was always in pain. Later I was to learn more about his pain. We were not getting along; everything was his fault or mine.

He left and moved to Texas with a family member. This lasted for a couple of years and once again we were back together again. We had no God in our lives even though we both knew about God. We did not have a church home and the devil was having a field day with us. At that point and time, we should have put God in control because of his love for us. There was no understanding. "Your hands made me and fashioned me, give me understanding, that I may learn your commandments." Psalm 119:73. Still unsure about our love and not thinking about the real love if God we continued in our relationship. Once again, I had not learned anything.

We bought a house and things were better, however, that old familiar feeling of unhappiness returned. We were not getting along once again, and he would leave without saying anything. I learned later he went back to Texas. Left alone in misery, about to lose the house, I was a mess and still didn't let God be my comforter. I told my parents and they prayed for us. Once again we talked and wanted to save our marriage and I agreed to let him come back into my life but the house was lost. Together with my two children we moved into an apartment to start over.

Things did get a little better as we were now communicating. I learned about his habits. He knew all about drugs and alcohol and women, not only had he been a pimp and did drugs, he sold them as well. I never saw him take medication, but I did know we could not keep any aspirin in the house. This was not normal. I did not know much about or the effects of drugs, but I would soon learn.

We still had a missing component in our life; which was God. We both belonged to different Christian churches in our early years before we met. We joined Victory Missionary Baptist Church where we became greeters and became faithful members. We were praising God, being thankful, and were doing well. He began complaining about his back pain, he went to the Veterans hospital and they gave him hydrocodone. He kept complaining about the pain and the doctors started increasing his medicine. We found that the over-counter medicine was not working for him anymore, and only the prescription medication would help. He was in denial about his addiction. He got so agitated and angry just talking about his addiction, that once again our marriage went array.

He didn't want any type of help, especially counseling, and he ended up leaving me again. What was I supposed to do? I didn't like seeing him in that condition and he did not want my help. I felt rejected, and I needed the help of the Lord. I became that paying woman. I knew God loved me and would see me through this. There is power in prayer and I knew it could turn the situation around. "Do not be anxious about anything, but in every situation, by prayer and petition, with thanksgiving, present your request to God. And the peace of God, which transcends all understanding, will guard your hearts and your minds in Christ Jesus." Philippians 4:6-7

Being in this marriage off and on for nearly seventeen years I began to strive for more knowledge about Christ. I took Evangelism classes for two years and was one of two Valedictorians of the class, receiving my certificate. A friend of mine was in training to become a Chaplain, invited me to attend her graduation. I was very intrigued by this and desired to know more about the Chaplaincy. I started taking classes at Messenger of Faith Ministries to become a Chaplain where I graduated as a Sr. Chaplain. "Study to shrew thyself approved unto God, a workman that needed not to be ashamed, rightly dividing the word of truth." 2nd Timothy 2:15.

I am now equipped to better help others through the word of God. My husband and I did get back together, and he is more addicted than ever. He was taking five and sometimes more pain pills a day. This became scary and out of control, I began praying for him, looking for a change in him to do better.
"Through whom we have gained access by faith into his grace in which we now stand. And we boast in the hope of the glory of God. Not only so, but we also glory in our suffering, because we know that suffering produces perseverance; Perseverance, character, hope. And hope does not put us to shame, because God's love has been poured out into our hearts through the Holy Spirit, who has been given to us" Romans 5:2-5.

We become closer together as time went on, building on relationship as we were now older, and then he was diagnosed with lung cancer. We were in disbelief. We could not believe what we were hearing from the Dr. What are we going to do? We were now closer than ever; this totally changed our lives. Our faith in God was stronger. He replied. "Because you have so little faith, Truly I tell you, if you have faith as small as a mustard seed, you can say to this mountain, move from here to there, and it will move. Nothing will be impossible for you" Matthew 17:20.

Having to nurture a sick husband day in and day out and maintain my daily activities wasn't easy. I was given strength daily by God, for he already knew the plan for me and how the Evangelism classes, the Chaplaincy classes, and the Ministry classes would be needed for me to face what I could not face alone. My husband passed away. Through all the mess that I created, the pain, embarrassment, all of those ups and downs God was always there. "Be strong and of good courage, do not fear nor be afraid of them: for the lord your God, He is the one who goes with you. He will not cleave you nor forsake you."

As a young woman I wanted love not realizing that I had unconditional love from God, and all that time He was in control. "Love is patience, love is kind, it does not envy, it does not boast, it is not proud, it does not dishonor others, it is not self-seeking, is not easily angered, keeps no record of wrong, Love does not delight in evil but rejoices with the truth, always persevere. Love never fails" 1 Corinthians 13:4-7.

As a widow I know that the presence of God is like a light that shines in us. God is love and helps us to know:

Love Is Understanding.

It is understanding the words unspoken.

Held back behind a veil of silence.

It is understanding the hurt,

Hidden beneath self-defiance.

It is understanding the joy felt,

On hearing your achievements.

It is understanding the longing,

The loneliness, the pain endured.

For, when you really understand,

The reasons behind the tears and fears.

The motives and the dreams,

The thought behind the actions,

The restrictions which influence.

And the desires of the Soul,

You can say, "I Know I Understand."

You can forgive anything, accept everything

---You can truly love!!

To God be The Glory

Amen

# Senior Chaplain Mary Moreau

Sr. Chaplain Mary graduated from Babylon Beauty School of Cosmetology, Long Island, New York in 1965. Mary won various awards in her chosen profession in her lifetime, was a member of the Hairdressers Association Guild and was a salon owner in Babylon Long Island and Queens, New York.

Mary graduated from River of Life Ministries School in 2012. Mary is a member and mentor of Hope Chaplains and an ordained Nevada Chaplin Corps USA, certified in CPR, AED and basic First Aid, member of the Mayor's Faith Based Initiative on Human Trafficking, member of Adopt a Cop Program, and member of Prayer Clinic.

Mary conducts sermons at Heritage Springs and West Care Women and Children Rehabilitation Center. She volunteers at various hospitals, hospice and rehabilitation centers, and providing chaplain services as requested.

Mary enjoys meeting people and serving the Chaplaincy as she loves the Lord and whole heartedly follows Matthew 28:19, "Go ye therefore and teach all nations, baptizing them in the name of the Father, Son and Holy Spirit.

# Chapter Twelve

# Love Is Never Failing

*By SR Chaplain Mary Moreau*

"When I was a child, I spoke as a child, I understood as a child, I thought as a child, but when I became a man, I put away childish things. For now we see in a mirror, dimly, but then Face to Face. Now I know just as I also am known." 1 Corinthians 13: 11-12

On an average day at Anthony's Beauty Salon I was placing a lady named Eleanor under the dryer. Yes, this was in the late 1980's – blow dryers and curling irons were not popular then. As I was seeing to her comfort, she took a little book out of her handbag. I said, "Eleanor what a small little book, what is it?" She looked up at me and said, "It's a Bible." (Basic Instructions Before Leaving Earth). I chuckled and said, "A Bible, may I see?" She handed me the Bible.

As I examined the Book, the cover said "New Testament". I opened it and there was Matthew, Mark, Luke, and John. I said, "I've never seen a small one. My Bible is big with "Old and New Testament on the cover". I handed her the book back, as I checked to see the temperature on the dryer. Eleanor looked up and said, "We are having a Bible study tonight, would you like to come?" I said, "Yes."

Later that night at Bible study I met some very nice people. This was something so different. At the end of the Bible Study, we all stood up, held hands and started to pray. Minister Jody Brown looked right at me and said, "Mary, do you know Jesus?" Looking right back I said, "Yes, I'm Roman Catholic." She walked over to me, held my hands and said, "Mary, do you know Jesus?" I said, "Yes, I'm Roman Catholic, of course I know Jesus."

Jody smiled, looked me right in the eyes as she placed her hand on my heart and said, "In your heart, do you know Jesus?" I placed my hand on hers and said, "Yes, I am Roman Catholic, I know Jesus!" She smiled gently and said, "Would you say this prayer with me?" I said, "If I don't agree with you I'm not saying it." She said, "Fine." She led me in the prayer of salvation which is almost like the Roman Catholic prayer of salvation, except she didn't mention the Pope of the Roman Catholic Church. Well, everyone was so happy; saving the angels were rejoicing for my Salvation.

"Just so, I tell you, there is joy before the angels of God over one sinner who repents." Luke 15:10

We all held hands and one by one each person started to pray. I said to myself, "This is good." Jody said, "Mary, may we get together? I would like to talk with you and go over some things in the Holy Bible; would you like that?" I said, "Yes." This was the end of the 1980's, the beginning of 1984, the beginning of a new relationship with Jody and Jesus. This relationship turned into a lasting friendship and an understanding of a "Love that never fails."

"Love never fails, but where there are prophecies, they will cease and know all mysteries and all knowledge; and if I have all faith, so as to remove mountains, but do not have LOVE, I am nothing."
1 Corinthians 13: 8,9

As Jody took me through the Holy Bible, the words started to take on a life of their own.

"There is power in the Word of God. In the beginning was the Word, and the Word was with God and the Word was God." John 1:1

In the midst of our studies of the Holy Bible, I would say to Jody, "I love Jesus." Jody would look at me and smile. She would say, "Do you know how much He loves you?" I would say, "He gave His life for me!"

"For God so loved the world that He gave His only begotten Son, that whoever believes in Him should not perish, but have eternal life."
John 3:16
Love is never failing…

Each day in our reading of God's Word, I started to understand. God's love is revealed to us through Jesus Christ. As my mind was being transformed through the words of Jesus' teaching, my understanding took on new life as the Holy Spirit led me into the truth of who I am in Christ and who Christ Jesus is in the Father God.

"For my Father and I are one." John 10:30

I see now when I told Jody, "Yes, I know Jesus, I'm Roman Catholic" that I spoke as a child. Now I have full knowledge of Jesus as a Christian and the relevance of the Holy Spirit. The Trinity is the core of Christianity.

Love is a letter from God professing His love.

"Love never fails. A new command I give, love one another as I have loved you" John 13:34

*With Love,*
*Chaplain, Mary Moreau*

# Chaplain Eva Jenkins

*May all your days be fulfilled in Christ. with love Eva J Kins* (handwritten)

Eva is a graduate of Lincoln Christian University. She currently practices as a Licensed Intern Marriage and Family Therapist and Drug and Alcohol Counselor in private practice at Power House Counseling. Having conquered depression, addiction & suicide, this petite powerhouse is focused on empowering others to become more than conquerors. She has spoken at churches and conferences, encouraging others to find the fire from within themselves. It is her hope to bring healing to broken-hearts, educating others about mental health & encouraging believers to stand strong in their faith.

She is currently working on a workbook to help others receive healing spiritually, relationally, & generationally called, Accelerate Your Faith. Find her personal testimony & learn basic principles to accelerate your faith in her upcoming book, Accelerate Your Faith.

Currently she is empowering women through Mary Kay, serving in Celebrate Recovery, facilitates Toastmasters at Florence Women's prison and teaches Biblical leadership to juveniles.

†Chapter Thirteen

## Confidence in Him

*By Chaplain Eva Jenkins*

In life we can put our confidence in many things. As children, we have our confidence in our parents to take care of us, we rely on teachers to guide us and we have counselors to help direct us. But let's face it, as we grow up we quickly learn people let us down, we cannot live up to other people's expectations and we end up becoming disappointed thinking that we cannot trust others. Over time we tend to diminish that inner voice that would protect us from doing things we may not have done but because we wanted to fit in or people please, we found ourselves doing things that went against our inner voice and ultimately our "true" selves quickly becomes jaded to the point we know longer know who we "truly" are. We believe what others say or have told us in which we lose a sense of how God sees us and become unsure of how He thinks about us.

To truly have confidence in God, it is in knowing who He is. We cannot believe other's opinions if we do not grow in relationship with who He is, otherwise how will you know how to trust Him? Our love does not come from ourselves. To truly love, we have to see His love for us. How can you know how special you are if hopelessness continues throughout your lonely days? How can you see Him rejoice over you if you are not experiencing joy? What confidence do you have in a loving God when everything seems to be against you? God is a Giver. Giver of life. Giver of finances. Giver of restoration. Giver of blessings. Giver of gifts. God has already provided everything for us in Christ Jesus. When you have received Him as your Lord and Savior, know the inheritance of eternal life, is your promise!

To know God has given you everything you could possibly ever need, is to be satisfied knowing He will give you everything in the right time and season. It is putting your confidence in Him even when your circumstances and situations may not be adding up, even when things seem like a mess, declare: "He is putting everything together". We stand on His word and truth that what we go through is for our GOOD. It is giving us the opportunity to walk by faith and not by sight, living out the hope of Jesus Christ who is inside of us.

We get to know what the Father is doing by the gift of the Holy Spirit and to be about our Father's business because He reveals to us what the Father is doing. Our confidence is in Him, in who He has made us to be to show the glory of who He is. But so often we do not want to wait on Him. We become impatient, we complain and become discouraged to the point we lose hope and faith and our confidence turns inward to what we believe "I" need to do. We mistake how Good God is because we compare Him to people, to earthly things and we lose sight in who we are because of society and what we have gone through in life. But when we keep Him as our focus, and lean not unto our own understanding we get to see Him at work in our lives. We become hopeful. We become confident in Him. We learn to trust again when we know He has His very best for us in His heart.

I was over having a boyfriend and knew I was wife material.
I broke up with a four year committed relationship to focus on God and what He had called me to do; share my testimony.
He started opening doors and I was getting ready to speak
at my first conference. He kept telling me how LIMITLESS He is.
I said, "Okay God, I get it, you're Limitless". I knew something was going to happen at this conference but never did I think I was going to meet my future husband.

I started praying for my husband in November 2013. My prayer was for God to give me His very best, whether he was deaf, blind or in a wheelchair. I believed God would give me His very best even if the person was deaf, blind or in a wheelchair. I did not care about the physical attributes of the person because God looks at the heart, and I needed a man after God's own heart, not based on what I have dated before. I had received a "friend request" from my husband to be, three days before I was going to speak at the conference.

I posted about the conference and how it was about seeking God first. He had messaged me about the conference and I invited him to come. The first night of the conference was a Friday evening when he walked into the building, God highlighted him out to me. I knew I needed to introduce myself. It was very brief; I introduced myself and told him I hope he has a good time.

After the conference that night, he told me how my testimony spoke to him. He came back the next day and since I was not speaking I told him I would sit next to him. We didn't say one word to each other. I left while he was still talking to the pastor. He messaged me that night and asked if I could give him a call. My thought was, "if I do not call him now, I never will". Our conversation flowed so much that I invited him to finish out the conference with me at the church.

Afterwards, he invited me to lunch and it was during that conversation that we both had learned that we have the same heart for the homeless attended the same university and had a ministry of healing. During that conversation God was telling me this is my "equally yoked partner". I told him I have been praying for my husband since November, and I believe God is telling me it's you. He then told me God had told him Friday night, when he got into his car after the conference, God spoke to him saying, "Eva is going to be your wife". He looked at me and said, "Well since we are going to get married, we might as well get to know each other".

Society tells us what to expect when we think about love, we see this in our music from the Oldies to Hip Hop, to country and Rap, we can see every genre of their story telling us how to be loved, how to get love and how to give love, especially in the movies. We tend to gain a misperception about finding that "one", who will satisfy all of our needs. We look, hunt and become unsatisfied with what is around or what we are experiencing that it makes us feel frustrated and settle in relationships. Then we give only half of ourselves because we have lost what it means to truly love.

To truly love someone is to know how to love ourselves. I have learned I cannot love myself without first loving God. When I focus all of my heart, soul and mind on God and His goodness, I find out how He sees me which makes me love myself the way He loves, flaws and all. It is quite amazing to know that our Loving Father made us ahead of time, knowing all the decisions and choices we are/were going to make. Although He has His best in His mind for us, we still have a will that allows us to choose His way or our own way. It's always a choice to love. When we become confident in Him, we learn how to love Him in obedience.

It took obedience for me to accept His way and deny my own wants for a spouse when it came to what "I thought" I might have needed. But God knew it wouldn't have led me to live the abundant life He has for me. Where there is faith, there is confirmation. A year before I met my husband I attended a Prophetic Conference at ICLV in Las Vegas. I received a word of knowledge, "God sees you as a string of pearls". At first I wasn't quite sure what this meant but it made me curious to learn about pearls. I found out they all are strong willed, well rounded and have been made over a few years through the process of having become irritant.

According to https:pearls of wisdom.thepearlsource.com/facts-about-pearls/how-are-pearls-made/:

Pearls are made when a small irritant that finds its way inside an oyster or mollusk. This can be a grain of sand or a piece of shell but is more typically a little parasite. This irritant bothers the mollusk, which then slowly secretes nacre to protect itself. Nacre is the substance that coats the inside of an oyster or mussel's shell. The nacre coats the irritant, and the layers build up over time.

Too often in life I know I have been an irritant! But even in that process, there is a promise: God is refining us to His likeness. Sometimes we do not change until there is pain in our lives. We do not seek Him until we are sick and tired of getting the same results. I fully surrendered when I was heartbroken, exhausted and done with doing things my way and chose to believe He has something better for me. I believed He is a Good Father who loves me and wants to give me everything He has written in His book for me. It was time to put my confidence in Him and trust that He has His best for me.

Exactly one year later from hearing that word of knowledge is when I met my husband and found out my husband is from Pearl, MS. I think God has a funny sense of humor.

Our love is in the choices we make, it doesn't happen by mistake. It's a conscious choice to move toward connection than allowing distance to take place. Love is not a loose term or feeling. Love is an action. Love is shown in what you do. To move in love, it takes courage, vulnerability and strength to fight against the grain. Your words could say you love someone but if you don't show it, do you truly love that person? Agape love is self-sacrificial. Putting aside your wants to meet the needs of others. Our love should be growing, even when it's painful.

Anyone can be disengaged or withdraw from a relationship, it takes using our freedom for the good rather than the bad when we're in Christ Jesus. To love God with all our heart, mind and strength is to love ourselves just as much. But we rarely do, which hinders the way that God sees us. We think God sees us as flawed, imperfect or incomplete due to our beliefs growing up and experiences but He made us whole, complete and wonderfully. There is no flaw in you.

Honestly, I have always been afraid of marriage but have always desired it. Not having a healthy marriage relationship model in the home, I have always thought I wouldn't measure up to the standard of a "happy home". But it was a fear implanted from my past that made me live out as though I could not get close to others due to my fear of abandonment. I became a self- saboteur and blamed others. I felt unworthy of love and did not know the love I was yearning for was implanted and rooted in Christ.

As my faith grew, I realized God would show me new ways on how to love. He has showed me to love others with an unfailing love, even when I'm mistreated, to not take revenge but to go to Him. When it's most difficult to love others, to pray for them. When I feel depressed or frustrated to go to Him in boldness, knowing I have access in the heavenly places. When thoughts of my past remind me of what I've given up, I remind myself the love of Christ and the newness of life He has given me. To know the love of Christ, which exceeds our knowledge is to receive the fullness of God in which we may be filled by His power, to work in us to show His glory. Our Father loves to give us good gifts. And it begins in who He is: LOVE.

"But blessed is the one who trusts in the LORD, whose confidence is in him." Jeremiah 17:7

"No one has greater love [no one has shown stronger affection] than to lay down (give up) his own life for his friends." John 15:13

For thus says the Lord GOD, the Holy One of Israel: "In returning and rest you shall be saved; In quietness and confidence shall be your strength." Isaiah 30:15

"For we are the circumcision, who worship God in the Spirit, rejoice in Christ Jesus, and have no confidence in the flesh"
Philippians 3:3

"By awesome deeds in righteousness You will answer us, O God of our salvation, You who are the confidence of all the ends of the earth, And of the far-off seas; Who established the mountains by His strength, Being clothed with power"
Psalms 65:5-6.

# Chaplain Karen Nickels

*God Bless Chaplain Karen Nickels*

Chaplain Karen is most definitely God's child. Originally from Plainfield, Indiana, attending Indiana State University, studying Arts and Social Work. Karen currently resides in Las Vegas, and she has a son named Travis..

Serving has obviously been her passion. She began a career at Delta Air Lines as a Stewardess and retired 34 years later. In 2007, Karen opened a home/gift store in Las Vegas, named Karen's Kreations and became a business woman. Karen is now retired. After an intense moment in 2003, she changed her focus about life and began to step-up in her faith. Dedicated to doing God's work she has served as a Community Group Leader, Wedding Officiate, Trauma Intervention Program (TIP) volunteer, and currently a H.O.P.E. Lead Chaplain at Centennial Hills Hospital. Licensed and ordained, she hopes to complete the Academy of Religious Studies at M.O.F.M. in February, 2019 and become a Sr. Chaplain in the spring.

†Chapter Fourteen

# Love Is A Message in A Vision

*By Chaplain Karen Nickels*

Ahh....to be given a brief and loving moment with Jesus!

John 14:21 NIV says, "Whoever has my commands and keeps them is the one who loves me. The one who loves me will be loved by my Father, and I too will love them and show myself to them."

In May 2003, I was projected into such a moment with Jesus. But let's go back a few years before that moment.

After retiring from a long airline career in Dec 2001, I moved from San Diego to Las Vegas. I left my home of nearly 17 years. I looked forward to finally enjoying some downtime. I'm originally from Plainfield, Indiana. Las Vegas, NV was not on my retirement list of cities, but God knew best. I felt forced to move due to financial restraints in retirement. Multiple, stressful events had happened in the few years prior to my retirement.

My childhood home life was reckless, as my father was an alcoholic. This caused some addictive, emotional, destructive patterns within me. Relationships were often difficult to maintain.

We sometimes copy what we see even if it is unhealthy. It's probably our use of free will that God gives to all. I made a lot of wrong choices. I had even gone so far as to give up on God after a bad relationship and tended to blame Him for my circumstances. Up until then Christ and church had played a very important part in my life.

I was in a physical and verbal abusive relationship. Travis's father had walked out on us a few months before he was born. Afterwards, I found myself in the midst of a divorce and raising a child by myself. He eventually gave up parental rights in exchange for no child support. I became deeply in debt raising a child alone. The emotional strain plus the overnight hours I flew consistently played havoc with my senses. I flew internationally for extra hours leaving me very little time with my newborn. I was not happy; I was left alone to raise this child. Eventually, I made my peace with God but didn't have a true relationship with Him until much later.

Flying during 9/11, I noticed that my job as an International Flight Coordinator had changed dramatically and became very uncomfortable. However, I always loved my job and found it difficult to leave even after 34 years of employment. Not expecting to retire, I was only given 4 days to plan a lifelong retirement. Compounding the stress, the airline downsized and later went into bankruptcy. Eventually it survived which ensured my pension. My Uncle in San Diego was like a father to me. My father had died at 61. My uncle died coming off of a triple bypass shortly before I retired. My dear and beloved mother had to be moved to a skilled nursing home in Indiana and died the month I retired. Shortly after that, my only sibling in Indiana and I had an explosive division after my mother died. We had not had a relationship for many years, especially after he had married some 30+ years ago.

I obviously felt I was a victim of so many circumstances. I continued to make wrong choices. As you can see, I had a laundry list of people that I had felt deserted me, hurt me, angered me and certainly didn't love me. God had forsaken me and left me all alone "to do the impossible by myself!"

"We can do all things through Christ who gives us strength." Philippians 4:13.

"Above all, keep fervent in your love for one another, because love covers a multitude of sins." ... 1 Peter 4:8.

I have to admit I harbored un-forgiveness to many times. Unwilling to let the hurt inside me go away, it grew and grew.

In May 2003, to my amazement, I found myself in a screaming ambulance being quickly transported to one of the trauma hospitals in Las Vegas. It appeared in my early mid- 50's, I had suffered a major heart attack. I was also in denial. My first thought, "God, why am I having this happen to me now?" Another thought, "I'm too young for this to be happening" and lastly, "God, haven't I suffered enough?" Little did I know I was within an hour of death which obviously was not to come to me yet. Christ had always had a piece of my heart but nothing like what was about to happen to me.

In the days to follow it was determined I would have to have bypass surgery. I ended up with quadruple bypass. I was supposed to have the veins attached while my heart was lifted out of my chest and still beating. Instead, I had been switched during surgery and placed on a bypass machine. It was almost a 6-hour surgery.

Of course, I was scared. My beloved Uncle had died of a triple bypass only a few years prior. My father also had died at 61 because of a heart attack. I was very alone as most of my family had disappeared or died. I barely knew anyone in Las Vegas and definitely no family. My son was away at school and couldn't get back because of finals, which I felt like at the time was a poor excuse. I love him dearly and came to understand he was scared too. "I FELT SO UNLOVED!" Nevertheless, I began to realize I was to bear this on my own and by myself.

"There is no fear in love; but perfect love casts out fear, because fear involves punishment and the one who fears is not perfected in love." 1 John 4:18.

Yet there was this inner voice that kept assuring me, "I was not going to die." God did send a couple of angels. They were Flt Attendant acquaintances, now friends, who lived in Las Vegas. Conni came later to the hospital to be there before and after my surgery and Sandra who had insisted on calling 911, when she

147

called me on the day of my heart attack; met me at the hospital. This probably saved my life as I wasn't thinking clearly. God did not leave me alone as Conni and Sandra stepped in as my family. God just knew how I desperately needed them to be there.

I was sent to another hospital for surgery and was in that hospital a total of 14 days. As I lay on the surgery table I could feel myself separating from my body. Like a bird, I began flying down an unlit, gray, large tunnel at warp speed. I was confused, as I apparently had no real body. I also wondered about the gray area. Maybe I was headed "to a not so friendly place" and "wasn't I supposed to see a bright light?" Finally, I landed on a cliff-like place with a very dim, sunny light far in the distance. Everything else was very foggy, weird, and desolate. I also didn't recall where I came from, loved ones or the circumstances by which I had come here. I was just there. I was feeling disoriented but glad I had arrived somewhere at least. I rested for the moment.

While being there, I began to feel an energy come upon me and the area began to glow. What seemed out of nowhere a voice gently called out to me. It was not condemning, but inquiring it said, "Have you loved enough?" It seemed to wait for my answer in a most affectionate, loving way but I couldn't speak. The voice was magnified in all directions and repeated. It was hard to describe where it came from. I just knew it was Jesus even though I saw no one. Then a vision of faces of people I had either not forgiven or had held distant from me appeared like photographs.

148

I found myself wanting to love each of them and begged and wept for a long time to be given another chance. At the time, it seemed like I had experienced the answer to a lot of questions and had learned a lesson of forgiveness leading to love. Suddenly, like a burst of light I was filled with what I now know as "agape love" for everyone and everything. It was so enticing. I wanted to stay and never leave. There were no boundaries, no hate, only warmth. It was unconditional, raw, pure love. I have never felt it since.

I knew I was feeling God's merciful, grace-filled and agape love passing through me. Then as suddenly as it had come upon me, it departed. It was indescribable! I had never felt that kind of love towards anyone especially, the ones I disliked. The next memory was being awakened by a nurse telling me my surgery was over and I was ok. I remember, I had a breathing tube and my eyes were taped shut. I thought, "I must have died." Then I realized I had returned to my present body and state of recovery in the hospital. She then put me back into a deep sleep. "I had survived!"

That night I believe, I had died to myself and resurrected in Christ. I talked with a nurse several weeks afterward, who was creating a documentary on heart bypass patients. She informed me; many of us had similar experiences whose hearts had been stopped. I still wasn't so sure what I had felt. But I did know it was not of this world.

Some were saying the voice asked, "If they had served enough", "had forgiveness", or "been truthful" to others. Mine appeared to be a message about loving others. Other patients, also like me were rather reluctant to talk about it for a long time. She also verified that there was a time during the surgery that my heart was not beating. I had to be transferred off to a bypass machine in the middle of the bypass surgery. My heart had evidently missed several beats.

I was not on a path of righteousness, I was a believer though. I see now where God was with me through it all. I also felt some things changed in me after this experience. It was slow in the beginning. I continued to make many mistakes but always moving forward in my faith. I felt compelled to go forward and research this new found faith and love that appeared to me in this vision. Only God can explain it, but great opportunities were placed before me as my health continued to improve rapidly. This was no accident. There were a lot of volunteer and service opportunities to honor the Father that came my way.

I had this urge to give back what was given to me. Simply… LIFE! I was obviously being given another chance. Energetically I said, "Yes" to serve God when I began to recover. A whole new and different world began opening up to me, a world of compassion. Years later I experienced re-baptism in the Jordan River in Israel. Something happened and changed me more, even after two prior baptisms. I repented of all my sins, asked for forgiveness and became accountable before entering the Jordan River. The warmth of love entered inside me that day. I felt it! It was another step I had not taken until then. I found a "personal relationship" with almighty God when this step was completed. Then I went to work for my new boss!

More followed......

Serving as volunteer in a hospital, I transitioned into (TIP) a Trauma Intervention Program which were called to death scenes and trauma. I was more empathetic, loving and caring to others. I found a new church that grew me in discipleship and knowledge of Him. As I faithfully attended, loving and caring relationships developed with other believers. Through this I volunteered as an audio/lyric tech, wedding/funeral attendant thus making me more responsible. This led to leadership in the church. I felt love as I loved what I did to help others, guiding them in the Word of the Lord. I think, He smiled and blessed me as He said, "it is good!"

Blessings... to become a Lay Chaplain volunteering with H.O.P.E. Chaplaincy in Las Vegas. I found myself in the hospitals, visiting with patients who were suffering. Love, hope and encouragement were now my new mission. I love being given the opportunity to serve others for Christ and not be a victim of my own choices.

Blessings... to be ordained and licensed as a Chaplain (MOFM) serving Christ anywhere and everywhere. God does work thru me by being His servant to others who are suffering or in need; I feel loved and able to love back. I've allowed him to make me His instrument. There is such a God-filled reward in this type of work, that it is indescribable. I love the people I meet and what God does through me daily from my brokenness! As it says in 1 Thessalonians 3:12, "And may the Lord cause you to increase and abound in love for one another, and for all people just as we also do for you."

The more I served the more I wanted to serve. It is out of love, I have that personal relationship with God, also the gift of the Holy Spirit who leads me. In 1 Timothy 1:5, "But the goal of our instruction is love from a pure heart and a good conscience and sincere faith." He informs us how to love in the spirit. I know the depth of the type of love God wants us to have with each other. It was a message revealed, to love all of you deeply with a pure heart. "Beloved, let us love one another, for love is from God; and everyone who loves is born of God and knows God." 1 John 4:7

God's choice for me is to spread this love as far as I can in this very broken world, and to make love contagious. To show the deep love and compassion of our Lord is an honor for me. After all, Jesus loved and died for us to experience that love. I was awakened from my years of complaining. I can say Jesus showed me the way.

"He is the way, the truth and the life." John 14:6.

I am never alone, he has my back. I just have to be a willing participant and agree to His choices for me and not rely on myself or others. Trust only in God. He does have your plan. May our loving Father message you today, to love deeply and forever!

Do you have the willingness to let that kind of love enter you?

If you do, then may you will also accept His invitation. It is there you will find Him! He is surrounded in His selfless and "agape love" for everyone!

# Chaplain Renita Clayton

Renita Clayton is a native of Berkeley California.

She is an ordained Chaplain, and serves as a Chaplain volunteer for RECAP; which is law enforcement and faith based community partnership and initiative.

She serves as a mentor for a local Las Vegas High School.

Renita is employed by the Clark County District Attorney's office in the victim witness assistance center.

She has served as the director of Servant Leader Training at her church New Antioch Christian Fellowship. Renita also serves alongside her mentor assisting churches in the area of leadership development.

Her goal in life is to give back to her community on a local level through serving as a Chaplain and a leader in the local church.

†Chapter Fifteen

# Love Is Always Present

*By Chaplain Renita Clayton*

It was the end of the school year in 1976; I was in the second grade and was looking forward to summer vacation as many children are each year. My mother and my Nana (who technically was my great aunt, but I will explain that later), came to meet with my teacher to pick up my final report card of the year. She shared with them that while I was definitely smart enough to move on to the third grade, she highly recommended that I remain in the second grade another year to give me a chance to mature emotionally. My life had been no picnic up to that point, but that was the first time I felt that there was something wrong with me and I felt so ashamed of myself because not only was there something wrong with me everyone else would know something was wrong with me.

My life was filled with turmoil from a very young age. My parents were in high school when I was conceived. My mother was a junior and my father a senior when I was born. I wasn't exactly planned just the byproduct of teenagers having sex. I lived in the house with my mother, her aunt and uncle and they raised me just as they were raising my mother. My Nana (my great aunt) and Godfather (my great uncle) never had children so they raised my mother. I lived in the house with them until my parents got married after I turned four years old and I moved in with my parents. My mother was a college student and my father worked, my father also sold drugs. I learned at a young age how to keep secrets.

My first secret I can remember having to keep was being molested by a kid in the neighborhood. I knew what was happening was wrong, but I was afraid that if I told someone I would get in trouble. I'm not sure why I thought I would get in trouble, but I held that secret and wished I didn't have to play with that particular kid. She was at least 4 years older than me and I'm not sure why we played together in the first place. My next secret was my parents had physical fights pretty regularly and they also sold drugs. I'm not even sure how someone so young knew that what their parents were doing was wrong, but I knew I was always told not to tell my Nana about anything that happened at my parents' house.

So, because I had to hold so many secrets, I developed into an introvert early. I was extremely quiet. I was so quiet that a teacher asked my Nana if I talked because I hardly talked and she told them I could talk and if they didn't believe it they would watch as we left school and they would see me actually talking to her. My Nana was my safe place and even though she was indeed the person that I felt most comfortable with and wished I lived full time with because her home was peaceful and I felt loved. I had to spend my time at my parents' house in my bedroom listening to them fight or entertaining their friends and customers.

I was raised Catholic and so I had an awareness of God and I remember always praying to him when I would drive home with my mother. I would pray that my father would not be home because I didn't want to see them fight. I can remember praying even in the midst of their fighting and my loneliness. Love was always present.

So, I shared that I had to repeat the second grade and while I was embarrassed to return to school still in the second grade and having to explain to all my friends in the third grade why I was still in the second grade, that second year turned out to be great! My teacher's name was Mrs. Graham. I'm not sure if she knew it was my 2nd time in the second grade, but because I already knew the material I felt like the smartest person in the 2nd grade! Mrs. Graham was especially kind to me and I felt really special when I was in school. My school days that year were great! Once again Love was always present because God certainly worked that situation out for my good!

Third grade brought probably the most heartbreaking year. My parents' fights were becoming more and more violent and my Nana decided to move to Louisiana to take care of her mother. My heart broke because there was no one to see about me and no one to see about my mother. I begged her to stay but she had to go, and so I begged to go with her, but my father wouldn't let me go. My Nana and Godfather were my safe place and the one place I could go where I knew I wouldn't have to worry about violence breaking out. It was a break from the stress and anxiety of living with my parents.

My father's family was around as well and I was close to all my uncles and aunt and cousins. My cousins were more like my siblings growing up and my Grandfather was a strong man and from what I was told he ran a very tight ship when my father and uncles were kids. My grandmother was a meek and mild woman. She cooked 3 meals a day and she was a teacher's aide at a local elementary school and she faithfully went to church. I enjoyed going to their homes, but it wasn't the same as being with my Nana. My father's family knew how explosive his temper was, but they always made excuses for his behavior.

My father was the oldest of his brothers so I'm sure they looked at him like he had it all together. I mean, he had a wife, owned his own home, and he had a great job, nice car, and a daughter. I spent most of my life not really liking my father. I thought he was mean because he would beat up my mother. I never even called him daddy or dad, I wouldn't call him anything. I barely spoke to him and I only responded to whatever he said to me. He never abused me, he was a good provider of material things, but he also didn't really care for my Nana. I think it was because she and her husband were my preference.

My family life became increasingly violent and in between the fighting my sister was born. The blessing was my Nana moved back to California so I had my safe place back. My parents eventually separated and finally divorced. Their violent outbreaks still occurred just not as frequently. We lived with my Nana full time once they were finally separated and I was happy about it.

I decided in middle school that I no longer wanted to attend Catholic school and requested to go to public school and my Nana allowed me to do that. I'm not sure what happened with me emotionally, on the surface I was living in a peaceful place, but at the age of twelve I attempted my first suicide. I took pills and left a note. My family responded by scolding me and telling me that people only do things like that to get attention and that I didn't need to do things like that for attention. They never took me for therapy or anything and I just continued to bottle up my feelings and suppress my emotions. Love was present even though I didn't recognize it, but love let me live because love knew that I had a greater purpose for my life.

My high school years were spent looking for acceptance and a place to belong. I was drinking heavily and making reckless choices. I thought I would find my place with the crowd I was hanging out with. We never went to class. I allowed guys to misuse me, but I still had this huge void in my life. I looked for a mother figure in others which often left me feeling rejected and unloved. I was slipping into a depression and didn't even know it and no one around me knew that I was in a bad place on the inside because I had learned how to master wearing a mask and because I was so quiet no one expected me to be so verbal about anything going on in my life. There was no particular event that had taken place in my life, but I did make my second attempt at suicide. I used drugs and alcohol this time and I left no note this time. I just wanted to go to sleep and not wake up. Since you're reading this I clearly woke up the next day. I remember being disappointed that I failed again at ending my life. There was love yet again saying I shall live and not die and declare the goodness of God.

I did go into counseling after my second attempt, but it didn't work out because I was so use to holding on to all my secrets because after all I was a teenager and no one knew I had been molested, no one knew the anxiety and fear that I had been living with as a child living with my parents and I certainly didn't want to go through the humiliation of being different I mean only crazy people go see therapist especially in the black community. So, therapy was very short lived for me because I just couldn't bring myself to open up.

I went on to graduate from high school by the grace of God because I certainly didn't spend much time going to class. It was love that really covered me because I do believe my Nana would have wanted to kill me if I hadn't graduated on time.

My young adult years were filled with even more drinking and even more reckless choices. I ended up falling in love with a man when I was 25 and he was 37. I fell in love quickly and hard. I wanted to be loved and accepted so bad I was willing to love a man that I had no business dating. He ended up being married but made all the promises married men make when they cheat on their wives. This relationship took me on a very emotional rollercoaster. So much so, that I attempted suicide for a 3rd time because I felt like if I couldn't be with this man, I had no purpose for living and I didn't want to live. Love was present once again and Love gave me yet another chance.

My best friend was always by my side and she really encouraged me to say Yes to God and to what He had planned for my life. So, I began really slow just spending more time reading my bible. I started going to the community college and I met a friend who was also a Christian. She and I really formed a tight bond and I learned how to have fun without drinking. My best friend, my new friend and I started a bible study group where we got together and prayed and studied the bible. We ministered the Word to each other and God really began to strengthen me. I learned how to forgive my parents and I came to understand that they did the very best they could base on their understanding of life. I continued to seek God and I even joined a church where I could grow. My entire way of life changed. I wasn't perfect and I still made mistakes, but I learned that God still loved me just as I was.

I reconciled my relationship with my father. He even gave his life to God and asked my forgiveness for how he treated me and my mother when I was growing up. He explained that he grew up watching his father treat his mother like that and he thought he was doing the right thing. My father has since passed away. I have to admit that I was very upset with God when he passed away because it was shortly after our reconciliation that he passed away and I felt like I was cheated out of having a relationship with him, but today I am thankful knowing that my father is with God and that we did have the conversation.

My best friend passed away as well and I was devastated at her passing, but I thank God that He used her to bring me back into relationship with Him. It was her example that she set that showed me it was possible to live for God and still have fun.

My life started out in a very traumatic and filled with fear, anxiety and depression, but the Love of God was always with me and God had a greater purpose for my life and He has allowed me to see that all I went through at such an early age was for His glory and He always had a purpose for my life. God showed me that He didn't make a mistake in choosing my parents, but He even had a plan in place to help me through the turmoil by blessing me with my Nana. He knew I needed her to survive so that He would be able to get the glory out of my life. God's word is true when He tells us in Romans 8:28 that all things work out together for the good of those that love God. In Jeremiah 29:11 For I know the plans I have for you," declares the LORD, "plans to prosper you and not to harm you, plans to give you hope and a future. Jeremiah 1:5 says Before

I even formed you in your mother's womb, I knew all about you. Before you drew your first breath, I had already chosen you to be . My prophet to speak My word to the nations.

God knows all about us and He knows every bad choice that we were going to make before we knew we were going to make it. We don't have to live in guilt and condemnation. If you take the time to look back over your life, I promise you will see where God was and that His Love never left you, it was his love that kept you alive and in your right mind.

Love was always present with me and God has always made a way for me even when I didn't know it was him. Love has always been present with you even when you couldn't see it or believe it. God has made a way for you as well.

# Chaplain PJ Belanger

PJ (PureJoy) Belanger attends Ignite Christian Center in Henderson. PJ served for 17 years as a small group leader through Central Christian Church and prior, had the awesome opportunity to study biblical research and teaching for 12 years coordinating home bible study fellowships and classes in five states.

PJ was ordained as a Chaplain in November 2017 through Messages of Faith Ministries. PJ serves, volunteers and advocates through community religious ministries and organization's such as Empowered Kingdom, Adopt-a-Cop, Hope for Prisoners, Americans for Prosperity, The Libre Initiative, Grassroots Leadership Academy, NORML, Patient to Patient, CNNA and Senior Spotlight Services and launching Civility Heroes.

PJ is a Certified Health Educator, Certified Wellness Educator and a plethora of other modalities and techniques.

PJ has two beautiful daughters and is Nana to five amazing grandkids! She is a master networker and community connector who has personally overcome 2 autoimmune diseases and mental health issues as she studied, practiced and taught natural healing, disease prevention and non-toxic living for nearly 40 years... planting seeds of love for hope and healing for the sick and hurting.

# Chapter Sixteen

# Love Is A Soft Heart

*By Chaplain PJ Belanger*

Miraculous, unprecedented and outrageous! That's what love is!

It truly is amazing that through all of the traumas and betrayals of life The LORD has kept my heart flexible and soft instead of allowing hard-heartedness to take over and rule over my life! Being hard hearted would be explainable, understandable and just about justifiable for my soul who has endured every type of child abuse imaginable, neglect, rejection, abandonment, burned, beaten, starved; left for days at a time as a toddler and young child with a bed full of dolls and books as a babysitter. Peril and danger were all around me since before my birth. I was even told at my very first ever female exam when I was 16, that I had survived an abortion attempt! It was detected by a certain enzyme present in my culture!

I remember at about the age of four, I believe; a little boy in the sand area in the apartments we lived in was breaking Coke bottles to watch the glass shattered! He bullied me, forcing me to throw one down too so he could watch and laugh! I got cut pretty bad on my finger and my foot that required stitches! I have the scars and

165

the memories of bleeding everywhere. I was not able to find help at home. No one was there. I remember getting swatted with a broom by the landlady for bleeding all over her stairs!

Then, fast forward with me for a bit, I went on to experience several unhealthy relationships, a failed marriage, four generations of domestic violence, mental health issues, battling to overcome 2 auto-immune diseases and being stalked by a murderer, my businesses crashed, loss of income, loss of homes, taken from and taken advantage of by a multiple of so-called friends and basically left with what 'seems' like NOTHING! Struggling with chronic homelessness, couch surfing for years, Moving your things from place to place every six months or so and living out of tote bags can wear out a tender soul... If I had let it! It's unnerving to not know where you have what, and what you have where!

However, I have fought and refuse to be defeated by the constant fiery darts of the wicked one! Lies of the enemy! The enemy of our God is our enemy. He hates me! That's for sure! Because I am a force to be reckoned with spiritually; I impact his kingdom by being a servant of love, light and hope for the LORD's Kingdom of righteousness! Satan has been trying to kill me since I was in the womb, before I was even born and so very many times since! He even tried while I was having both my babies! He tried to kill me and them. BUT GOD has other plans for me!

The distractions and disturbances and disruptions that he has attempted to destroy my life with have been constant and the attacks on my mind have been deliberate! The self-doubt, worthlessness an confusion have brought consistent distress. Under distress it is far more challenging to move forward in life. That is the goal of this realm and it's cohorts. Proactive positivity has been my countermeasure to overcome emotionally and mentally feeling very miss wired and damaged. It has been a daunting task to say the least!

" I don't matter"; "Nothing ever works out for me"! These are the thoughts that played over and over as recordings to torment me day after day after day; relationship after relationship! An 'ideal' life was not in the cards for me! However, I would still rather be me whom The Father has pursued, cared for and blessed continually then to be someone who is without Him! In spite of feeling like an outright failure most of the time, I had to endure to push through and go on bravely! After all; I had two daughters to raise and try to be a good example for! Ugh!

All the while, inadequacy and self-hatred from so much abuse, mistreatment and being misunderstood most all of the time it seemed, was causing quite a painful confounding existence. But, The LORD ABBA, Father God has faithfully delivered me through it all every time. It is His call upon my life that made me aware that my life has purpose. He has a plan! Seeking His will and Love have been a life raft in a sea of devaluing, devastating marginalization of my truest and highest self!

Although this world has done everything; and I do mean just about everything, to thwart my identity in Christ and keep me wallowing in feeling like I was unacceptable and unlovable; God's Word tells me something different! His love has showed me something different! I Am His Beloved! I was just about convinced that no one could ever tolerate me and that I was just too much for anyone to be able to handle or deal with. This is just not true! The love of Christ Jesus to die for me proved it! That is what I am sure of now! God has established great worth in and through me and my life!

I was a little girl, about 9 years old, when He made His Presence known to me! The courts had decided to put me up for adoption after years in foster care. I underwent a series of tests at the Children's Hospital and met a few couples. I still have a picture of myself from one day at the medical center with a big huge smile. It seems like my eyes were saying: "Pick me'! 'Pick me!" Somehow however, my foster parents were granted legal guardianship. That's when my social worker stopped visiting to check in on me and the random molestation in the middle of the night in my sleep began! That is also when mental and emotional abuse were inflicted upon me by them stirring things up against me and blaming me for everything between me and the other foster kid siblings especially when they would violate me. I was made to feel like nobody cared about me, nobody would look out for me and that I was once again, unwanted. In His sweet holiness, He made sure I knew that He was looking out for me! The wooing of my Creator has been so obvious to me that it has enabled me to press forward toward the mark of His high calling and to move on and get over this present evil realm! His companionship and the development of this sacred spiritual relationship with my Savior Christ Jesus have been my driving force to live, to do more than just survive, but instead to push through keep going and rise up! I believe beyond a shadow of a doubt that we were not born for mediocrity and there is absolutely nothing normal about me! He has Destined me for His Greatness!

All I have ever wanted in life, my greatest desire has been to be a glory to God ever since He opened His heart in the Scriptures to me, unlike anyone else I saw around me when I was about 20 years old! You see, I had been pleading with God for a couple years at this point for Him to tell me 'why I was alive'? 'Why did He put me here'? I told God repeatedly He had to show me why I was here or I else was going to kill myself. I did want not to live! I kept all this in as I partied pretending to be happy! Until He nudged me and brought me to my truly divine purpose for life and living! To be loved by Him! And, to help others find this hope that unconditional love brings! I have come to the reality that I was not having delusions of grandeur but rather divine desires of the heart being revealed to me so that His greatness that I'm destined for can become my theme instead of all of the negatives that have been perpetrated against me and my mind. His greatness shining through my life for my life and my life is my destiny!

Knowing this now, that I have eternal Kingdom purpose; I have had an incredible propeller through oppressions, injustices, and traumas of all sorts. The encouragement and uplifting that I have received from His Word, His promises, His people, His care, concern, provisions, healing and continually established hope have nurtured me! He has taken me from the defeated and suicidal teenager Patty (Patty Jane) to the now, Beloved woman of God; to PJ (PureJoy / Praising Jesus)! Recently I was given the Word from The LORD that He says PJ stands for "Precious Jewel as in a signet ring He would show off"! Such deliverance He has afforded me! That's what Love Is... it is help and a shield! The more I have learned to trust in His holy name and to rejoice and to praise Him no matter what is going on around me, the more I am supplied with sympathetic relief, goodwill tolerance and a soft heart!

Fact of the matter is I am only still alive and living due to His love! His love has tracked to me. His quest for me has been my sustaining courage to overcome and to keep going on. The capacity to cope with this evil realm as well as the tenacity to shine in the darkness is His vital gifts to me. His orchestration of things and places and people on our behalf are my fortitude to grow and to learn and to change into His likeness. To be content has been challenging! To stop complaining is crucial. Focusing on a walk worthy of His calling has consumed me. Love is this incredible life

I get to live despite all the demonic life threatening events that have plagued me since my conception!

His Excellency has uplifted me and repeatedly delivered me from death and destruction of the enemy. On my worst days He has always been brilliant! His love is so merciful and magnificent that it covers all my humanity and weaknesses! His forgiveness elevates me in spite of my unfaithful fears that have caused tumultuous panic and unbelief! His covering is my encouragement. It builds me up. His grace, His mercy, His favor and blessings provide true rest for my weary soul to find strength and ability and authority to prevail and claim all the favor and victories and blessings that Jesus' blood paid for me (and for You)! Drawn to authentic intimacy with Holy Spirit has developed a victorious harvest of righteousness, elevated confidence and delivers a fulfilling peace to live in joy regardless of the harrowing unfortunate childhood and disconnected life. His love is truly the only real love I've have ever really known!

The LORD of all has closely cared for me in spite of myself, my perception of my life and the horrific atrocities inflicted upon me. The Father of Lights has always been there for me! Shined up on me! He has never left me alone even if I am upset and want Him too. He always shows up as purpose and or provision! He is my song, my joy, my strength to endure and to overcome! That's what Live Is! Extravagant! His garish love has gotten me through good days, bad days, overwhelming days, too tired days, I am awesome

171

days, I can't go on days and let me still show up every day! I have found His love to be inescapable because He has purposed in my heart to desire Him! I so desire to know Him and to be known of Him! Even whenever I am downtrodden or overwhelmed or agitated and want to be mad at God; it is all that I can do to not turn to Him. It is in my very being now to turn everything over to Him, to cast my cares upon Him knowing how much He cares for me! "casting all your cares [all your anxieties, all your worries, and all your concerns, once and for all] on Him, for He cares about you [with deepest affection, and watches over you very carefully]." 1Peter 5:7

I am so very grateful for an inherent and incessant passion to fulfill my divine purpose as an ambassador for Christ Jesus my Savior! This providential vocation that He has purposed for my life defies logic and has been exhausting as I have allowed the devil to play yo-yo and push me pull you with my identity! However, since it is based on His abilities and not mine, I am and will forever be His chosen one! This super natural reality has allowed me to be a lot saner than I have a right to be!

ABBA Father has faithfully magnified brilliance in my life while mental malfunction limited my perceived choices. Yet, He has arranged incredible relational, educational, emotional and professional antidotes to being insane constantly for me. In spite of feeling horribly flawed and unqualified to fulfill my destiny, He has called me to plant seeds of love for hope and healing for the sick and hurting to find wholeness like He has provided me! It is my mandate: I am an Agape Sower! Wholeness is what we crave! It is what we need! It is what God wants for us and it is what He paid for us with Christ's blood! Trails will always come and go. Storms will always blow. But God's love stands strong so I can stand on His promises of victory that bring Him glory and help others do the same! To be at-one (atoned) with our creator and Father is empowering despite being broken, scattered and intimidated to be myself!

Due to experiencing so many hardships and tormenting abuses that have been nearly crushing and astounding; I have been hindered by a lifelong battle with my self-confidence and self-esteem. Through the washing of the water of His Word I have learned Godfidence! His promises have become my thoughts by contemplating His goodness! This has been a very effective tool to transform my mind. I do no allow my mind to talk to me any longer! Instead to let me focus on whom He made me to be and what He says of me so that I may live and be a resemblance of a stable life! This has been His energizing love for me displayed in a tangible way! Love from heaven, not for heaven, is what brings deliverance to my heart, my mind and my life!

I have had the amazing privilege of seeing kingdom realities in manifestation in the here and now many times over the years and decades! What a good good Father! Captivated by His love for me I am restored and He replenishes me. I am beyond honored to worship Him. I stay anchored to the hope of the return of our King of Kings and Lord of Lord's! In the meantime, I know that I know that I know Daddy's sweet tender directing and His unceasing pursuit; give us a perspective of his Holiness so that we can sense His love and presence. His habitual rescuing of my heart, my mind and my life has made His Love remarkable and distinctly authentic!

# Chaplain Ronda Moppert

Ronda Moppert was born in Las Vegas and has spent her entire life here. She is a mother of five sons and considers being their mother her greatest accomplishment.

Ronda is an ordained Chaplain. She has also studied at Liberty University on-line programs.

Ronda has taken part in the community through the Adopt A Cop NV Ministry and the LVMPD Take Back the Strip initiatives.

Ronda's faith has grown stronger every day after the traumatic event in which she almost died from ten years ago.

Every day Ronda has been shown by God that He is not done with her yet, and she has so much more to achieve in life.

# Chapter Seventeen

# Love Is Enduring

*By Chaplain Ronda Moppert*

Summer is my favorite time of year, especially because I love to take summer vacations with my kids. Who doesn't like to go on vacation? They are filled with memory making moments of families traveling to far off places or just escaping the everyday routine of their lives. In July of 2009, I was planning to spend a few days with my kids away from our everyday routine and have a stay-cation. Not too exciting but I was raising 5 young boys, my oldest had just turned 10 and my youngest son was just 10 months old, so travel was really out the question. We were scheduled to do fun stuff around town, movies, swimming and bowling.

Late July in Las Vegas is hot. Not 100 degrees hot more like 120 degrees hot and the apartment where I was living with my kids never seemed to cool off. When our cousin Sundae invited us to stay at her apartment for a few days and enjoy the pool, we jumped at the chance. My sons love the water; I have always thought they were not half Hawaiian but half fish. We spent that first day off swimming and enjoying Sundae's cable TV. I also needed to escape the boiling situation with my husband, Shannon.

Shannon had always been abusive but I let myself be talked into allowing and accepting his behavior for the good of my kids. Kids do better in a household with two parents, all the studies say so. Being at Sundae's apartment was really the only place he allowed me to have peace, anywhere else and he would have went ballistic. This was my SAFE PLACE. The last few weeks he had gotten more and more abusive. There was not a moment when I wasn't on guard and on watch from what he might do to me. During this time he had even broken into my house more than once.

On the day before, Shannon had even attacked me at work. I was pulling into work on a typical Saturday morning. I pulled into the parking lot and watched as all of my co-workers walked inside the building. I was just a few minutes later than I usually was, I grabbed my lunch and phone and headed across the parking lot, I didn't get 30 feet from the rear of my car before I was pulled from behind and slammed to the ground. I don't remember being punched, I know I was kicked and stomped on because for weeks later I had a bruise on my upper arm that looked like a print of my husband's shoe.

A man and woman watched from across the street, I could hear them yelling and as quickly as the attack had begun, it had ended. The couple ran across the street to help me and I could hear the woman on the phone shouting to the police, but the thing that stands out in my mind is the laughter that I heard from my husband as he was driving away from the scene.

That Saturday morning attack was not the first time that my husband attacked me. It was just the first time that he had done it out in public with so many witnesses. I worked that day. I had too. I had to pretend that everything was fine. I had been doing that for so long that "it's fine" was my normal emotion to it all. I was never happy, sad, or angry. No, I was fine. If my emotions were something other than fine it could be used against me. Who wants to admit that their whole life is in chaos?

That Saturday night, I went back to Sundae's apartment. I had spent so many nights on her couch that her tiny apartment had begun to feel like a second home. I brought my kids straight back to her apartment to pretend that everything was alright. It was fine. Everything was fine. If I said it enough times then maybe everything would be fine. Everything would be fine I repeated.

We spent the next day swimming as I had previously planned. I did not want them to think that I could not keep a simple promise. The kids swam, watched cable TV, played computer games and I made one of their favorite dinners, taco salad. Everything was made to make them believe that everything was fine. My sons had no idea what was going on inside of my head. I felt so stuck and helpless. I felt that God had left me.

Later that evening, Sundae and her Son came home from their weekend trip. We all settled down and eventually fell asleep. But not for long, at about 2am that morning, Shannon came crashing through the front door.

I remember being thrown from the couch I was sleeping on and onto the tile floor. There was so much pain. It came suddenly and without warning from all over my body. I could feel warmth flowing all over my body. And then I could hardly breathe. Each breath caused my whole body to burn in pain. I looked up and saw six pairs of eyes. My sons and my nephew stared down at me in shock and disbelief. They simply could not believe what they had just seen.

I drifted in and out of consciousness. I remember being pushed through the hospital, seeing the lights overhead as they seemed to pass by me, one after the other. Nurses and doctor were talking quickly and giving information and instructions on how to save me. One nurse looked down and into my eyes, "Ronda, while you are here your name is Trauma Hazel. Do you understand? You have to say yes."

"Yes." I whispered in hushed tones. I could barely hear my own voice in my head. My thoughts were so cloudy. I called out to God. God please forgive Shannon for doing this to me. I don't know if I will live or die but I forgive Shannon for what he has done to me. I know God that I have done so many bad and evil things, please forgive me. I do not hate Shannon for what he has done. I know that You and You alone Lord will handle Shannon.

And I slowly began to drift away from myself. I could see myself laying there in that hospital room. I could see the doctors and nurses attending to me. And then suddenly I was no longer there.

Somewhere, I was somewhere else. I was in a place I had never seen before. I wasn't in a room or outside, I was in a space that was filled with light and soft warmth. In front of me were three people who had meant so much to me but had all passed on. I could not touch them. I could not feel them. They were just staring at me. Not saying anything, almost like they could not.

My father had died when I was 19 years old; he looked at me with just a small tear in the corner of his eye. He never cried but he would often get choked up in this way and that small tear would form but never ever leave that eye. Elaine, a dear and close friend, who had died about 4 years earlier, stared and me shook her head. She had done this to me many times over the years and always as a sign that I could do better and always made me feel like I deserved better than what I had gotten. And the last person that I saw surprised me the most, Jean. She was my husband's stepmother. She could barely look at me as she shared in the pain that I was in.

All around me my life played out. I saw scenes from my childhood, and my adult life. All at once and it was almost too much to take in. In that moment, I heard this voice, "Not now. It's too soon." I knew I would survive, the very least that I would not die. Not that day.

Survival was all about the physical fight at first. I refused to be held down. I spent 7 days in a trauma room in Sunrise Hospital.

On that eighth day, I met with a doctor who began to tell me about each and every injury. Both of my lungs had been punctured. My left lung had a tube placed in it to drain all the blood that had collected there. I had injuries to my stomach and liver. I had defensive wounds on my right hand and my right thigh. I was covered in bruises and had also suffered from a concussion. I had been stabbed in back lower back and 1 centimeter is all that had separated me and my ability to ever walk again. He told me how lucky I was. Yea, I thought that long list of injuries sure sounds like I was lucky.

I was moved to a regular hospital room and after just 11 days, I was released out into the real world to try and get my life back. I did not know what my life even looked like anymore. I had been told that Shannon had been arrested that same night as the attack and was in the Clark County jail. He was on suicide watch. I kind of found that funny. He wanted to kill himself for what he had done to me. Because of this attack, I had lost custody of my children. But lucky for me the courts and judges knew what was happening and I got them back right away.

I lost my faith in God when I was 19 years old when my father had died. I really thought that God had abandoned me because He had taken away my earthly father. But in that hospital room as I watched the scenes of my life play all around me, I knew that God had always been with me. Jesus never walked away even when I turned from Him. He was there through every moment of my life because He showed me He was. I saw flashes of what my life was and what my life could be. My life was not meant to be lived imprisoned in a relationship filled with pain. But I was meant to live a full life filled with His blessings and happiness.

The road to those blessing however is not an easy one. Every day I live with remembrance of that July day. It has marked me in so many ways. My children have never been the same since that day. Before July 20, 2009, I tried to do everything in the world to keep the peace and calm with my husband.

Every day after that day, I have lived for me and my sons. I have not thought about what Shannon might think about this. No, I think Jesus is the leader and Lord over my life and He is the only one that matters. In Psalms 136, the psalmist writes, His faithful love endures forever. God has kept His promise to love me through each and every part of my life, even when I thought He had abandoned me He was right there with me.

# Chaplain Beverly Weesner

Beverly J. Weesner is a minister and Bible Scholar. She graduated from Valley Forge Christian College in Phoenixville, PA. Her major was Ministerial; minors were Child Education and Music.

Together with her husband, Alvin O. Weesner, Beverly has ministered as Pastor and Evangelist for 58 years throughout the nation. In conjunction with his preaching, she played saxophone, sang and held children's meetings prior to their regular services.

She has also done chalk drawings to illustrate sermons.

In 2004, she wrote a poem entitled, "The Maestro" which won international recognition, and was awarded first place. It was the first poem on page 3 of the 2004 Touch of Tomorrow, of the International Library of Poetry.

She and her Husband, Al, have written and published six books that are available through Amazon.com, which can be ordered through their

website: www.weesnerbooks.com.

Beverly also ministers with her husband in Healing Rooms, Hope for Prisoners as a mentor, The Mayors Faith Initiative on Human Trafficking and on the Board of Directors of a Brothel Ministry.

†Chapter Eighteen

# Love Is A Miraculous Healing

*By Chaplain Bev Weesner*

"Do not fear, for I am with you; do not be afraid for I am your God I will strengthen you I will help you I will hold on to you with my righteous right hand" (Isaiah 41:10)

It was 5 a.m. when I was awakened by a strange feeling in my chest. My first thought was to monitor my pulse and blood pressure. The result of that action revealed to me that it was time to check in with a doctor. My heart was beating rapidly.

It just so happened that my husband, Al and I had an appointment with our podiatrist that morning at 9 a.m. In the same building as our doctor's office were several other doctors, so I asked if I could see a doctor regarding my heart. By this time I was feeling faint, and trembling.

I was immediately sent to a doctor who checked my heart and instantly told me to go to Urgent Care. So instead of going to our podiatrist, Al drove me to Urgent Care, where I was quickly sent to an examining room, given a gown and made ready for further examination. I was also hooked up to a heart monitor and prepped for blood drawing and medicine input.

It must have been 2-3 hours that I laid there, during which time chest x-rays, drawing blood, and other tests were being done, along with other careful monitoring.

Then, as it always seemed to happen, nature was calling me to the bathroom. I told the nurse that I needed to go to the bathroom, so she unhooked me, then left, coming back with a wheelchair. I asked her if I could walk. After a little persuasion, they agreed to let me walk, warning me to be careful and walk slowly. I had no problem getting to my destination.

When I was leaving the bathroom and walking back to the bed, I felt God's presence with me. I began to thank him for helping me, and as I walked, I felt compelled to walk faster.

Suddenly such a feeling of well-being came over me, I began to walk faster and take longer strides. I knew that God had healed my heart.

When I got back to the room and the doctor came in, he checked my heart and asked how I felt. I told him I felt very good. He then told me that my heartbeat was normal. After further examination he told me that I could go home.

Al had gone to eat lunch at a nearby diner, so I went to the hospital waiting room. I had not waited very long before a good friend came in to see how I was doing.

When he saw me in the waiting room, he was amazed that I was being released so soon. He told me he would take me home. I was able to contact Al and tell him I was on my way home.

What a mighty God we serve. He provides for every need.

# Chaplain Al Weesner

Alvin graduated from Valley Forge Christian College in Phoenixville, Pennsylvania and earned his BA degree in the Theology from Central Bible College in Springfield Missouri. He and his wife, Beverly, have pastored churches in Massachusetts, Colorado and Maryland. He also drove an 18 wheeler truck for eleven years.

Alvin is a retired pastor. He and Beverly are currently serving as chaplains in the Las Vegas area. They pray for the sick at the healing rooms in Henderson and Las Vegas. They also serve as mentors for Hope for Prisoners.

He and his wife have written and published six books that are available through Amazon.com. They can be ordered through their website also www.weesnerbooks.com.

Al is a US Navy veteran who was awarded the Warriors Medal of Valor. Other ministries he serves in are, director of a brothel ministry and the Mayor's Faith Initiative on Human Trafficking.

†Chapter Nineteen

# Love Is Being A Miracle

*By Chaplain Alvin Weesner*

(This is the exciting completion of my miraculous healing testimony as written in the chaplaincy book Jesus Is on page 124.)

We were attending the International Church of Las Vegas (ICLV) for a short time prior to the accident that shattered my femur and forced me into a wheelchair.

After flying back home from Denver, Colorado to Las Vegas Nevada it was good to get back to our home church ICLV. We had really missed it. That Sunday morning we heard our Pastor Paul Goulet announced that on Sunday evening he was having a healing service. We attended that healing service. When Pastor Paul called those who needed a healing to come up front, Bev, my wife, pushed me in the wheelchair to the altar area.

Pastor Paul came to me and asked if I thought I could walk. I said, " I don't know I haven't walked unassisted for six months."

He suddenly laid both hands on me and loudly proclaimed, " IN THE NAME OF JESUS ARISE AND WALK !! "

I leaped out of that wheelchair. Pastor Paul took me by the hand and we both walked back and forth in the altar area, Praising the Lord!

They put my wheel chair up on the platform for the rest of the service. Bev and I walked back to our seats unassisted.

After the service, I walked back up to the platform to retrieve my wheelchair. Pastor Joel Garcia asked me what I was going to do with it? I responded, "I'm going to push it out to my pick up truck."

I have never sat in it since! I actually gave it to a lady that needed it. As of this writing, it has been 20 years, and I am still completely healed!

God is no respecter of persons. He will heal you too. Here are a few healing scriptures that I have paraphrased to help your faith.

Proverbs 4:20-22
The word of God is life to all of my flash.

Exodus 23:25
I serve the Lord and healing is mine.

Psalm 103:3
I receive the benefit of God's healing.

Psalm 91:16

I will live a long life.


Isaiah 53:5

Jesus for myself and my sicknesses.


John 10:10

The devil comes to kill and destroy, but Jesus came to heal and give life abundantly.


John 1: 2

God's highest desire is for me to prosper and be in health and whole.


One Peter 2:24

Jesus has already paid the price for my healing.


Romans 8:11

The Spirit of life is making my body alive.


Psalm 107:20

God's word is healing.


Nahun 1:9

My sickness shall leave and not return.

# GOD WANTS YOU WELL!!!

The Lord can heal by a touch, by a word, and by physical anointing. He healed those close and at a distance. He healed on the Sabbath (any day will work); He healed individuals and groups.

There were seven cases where a demon was cast out. On eleven occasions friends brought the sick person to Jesus. On six occasions the sick person asked for healing himself. On three occasions the Lord performed the healing while at a distance; He healed eight persons up close with a touch. He healed seven simply by speaking a word. Three were healed when he spat and touch them. In one instance he healed through a gradual cure (John 4:52?He began to amend ... ")

How is He going to heal you? God wants to heal you someway, somehow. Reach out and allow him to touch you today. Don't let go, don't give up, He will heal you.

MY PRAYER FOR YOU:

Father, I stand in agreement, in the name of Jesus, for this person in need of healing. As they pray this prayer, I believe in faith with them, that every sickness, disease, infirmity, whether physical or emotional, will be healed. Amen!

# Love Is

## Graphics Acknowledgement

### Special Thank You to Chaplain Matt Ellenson

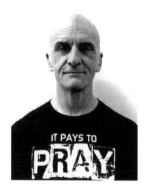

Matt is an ordained Chaplain, Artist, and Graphic Designer.

Made in the USA
San Bernardino, CA
27 April 2019